NATIVE AMERICANS

JAMES LAGOMARSINO

NATIVE AMERICANS

JAMES LAGOMARSINO

Published 2004 by Grange Books
an imprint of Grange Books PLC.
The Grange
Kings North Industrial Estate
Hoo nr. Rochester
Kent, UK
ME3 9ND

www.grangebooks.co.uk

All enquiries please email info@grangebooks.co.uk

ISBN 1-84013-727-4

Printed in China.

1 2 3 4 5 08 07 06 05 04

CONTENTS

INTRODUCTION

The history of the American native peoples is a long and fascinating one. The issues of who they are and where they came from have become the centre of attention for many studies. From simple enthusiasts to learned scholars, people have spent anything from hours to years trying to find out more about the subject. Young and old alike are caught by the allure of native Indians and their cultures. There are so many different aspects - from folklore to hunting skills, that there is surely something wonderful to be learned by everyone who shows an interest.

Sadly, the full story of the native peoples will never be known as many vital facts have been lost in the mists of time. Many cultures became extinct through disease or warfare well before the arrival of European settlers.

There are many different theories as to where the native American peoples came from, as well as exactly how they made the journey. The most widely accepted hypothesis is that they travelled from Asia into Alaska via Russia. Today the two continents are separated by a shallow sea known as the Bering Sound. During the last ice-age - which was approximately 20,000 - 30,000 years ago, however, the falling sea levels formed a land-bridge. This stretched from north-eastern Siberia into Alaska, making it possible to cross over on foot. Other theories suggest that the first settlers actually arrived on boats across the seas rather than by land. If this was the case, the most likely routes would be from Polynesia across the Pacific Ocean, or from Scandinavia across the northern Atlantic Ocean. It is possible that the ancestral Americans came via both methods.

There is a third theory, which is that the natives were always there from the start. Although there is no physical evidence that this was the case, many tribal cultures have legends which state that they were created in their homelands at the beginning of time.

It is likely that the land bridge was uncovered and recovered by the changing sea levels many times during the last ice-age. If this was the case, it would account for the fact that there were probably several different waves of migration. The common physical features demonstrated by the many different tribes or nations of native Americans indicate that they have the same origin. The many different languages spoken by them, however, would suggest that they arrived at different times. If there were several distinct migrations, it would help to explain the linguistic variations and complexity seen today.

As each wave of migration across the land bridge occurred, the new immigrants spread out from Alaska, going east and south into Canada and beyond. The popular view was that at least three separate migration waves occurred - this was inferred from a mixture of archaeological and anthropological evidence. Since then, however, population genetics has shown that there were four major periods of migration, with many smaller events in between. The vast majority of the migrants were from Asia, although genetic evidence seems to suggest that at least some of them came from Europe.

It is generally accepted that the first wave, which constituted the oldest Indian cultures in North America, was led by the Sandia peoples. There are some, however, who believe that they were pre-dated by as much as 10,000 years by earlier civilisations.

The Sandia culture existed around 15000 BC, and about three thousand years after this came the Clovis people at around 12000 BC. During this era - known as the late Pleistocene epoch, large mammals such as woolly mammoths and giant sloths provided good hunting for the early settlers. By the time the Folsom culture developed around 8000 BC, most of these massive creatures had died out. Just how much hunting by humans contributed to their demise is a subject of hot debate amongst scientists today. The Folsom peoples were primarily bison hunters.

The second wave was comprised of the Athabascan peoples - they were the early ancestors of many of today's better known tribes, such as the Navajos and Apaches. The third and last major immigration wave was made up of the Inuits, the Yupiks, and the Aleuts. Since the world's sea levels had gone up considerably since well before this occurred, the Bering land bridge had long since disappeared. Whether they crossed by boat or not is not known - since many of them are skilled in the use of the kayak it is highly likely. These late arrivals were so different from the those of the two earlier migration waves that they are often classed separately. As a result they are not normally be considered to be included in the term 'native American Indians'.

It was not long before the migrating peoples had established thriving cultures - these fell into seven basic geographic regions north of Mexico. These are the Arctic and Sub-Arctic, the North-west Coast, the Plains and Prairie, the Plateau and Great Basin, the North-east, the South-west and the South-east.

When Christopher Columbus arrived in 1492 the continent was sparsely populated. Some say that there were as many as 10 million people living north of Mexico, although it is likely that the figure was closer to 2 million. Either way, for such a big land mass, this was a small population. Unfortunately, the Spanish explorers and those Europeans that followed brought with them dreadful diseases such as smallpox, chicken pox, influenza and measles. As the native American peoples had not been exposed to these virulent sicknesses before, it had a catastrophic effect on them as they had little or no immunity. Within the first hundred years of contact with Europeans, tens of thousands of them died as a result of disease. Some estimates suggest that more than 80% of certain native Indian populations died in these terrible times.

When Christopher Columbus first reached the shores of America, he was actually looking for the East Indies - thinking that he had found them, he called the natives

INTRODUCTION

'Indians'. This name stuck, although there are many variations on the term. Alternatives include Amerindians, Amerins, Indyans, Injuns, or Red Indians. It is a controversial subject, and as political attitudes change, so the 'correct' terminology varies. The most popular names in the United States are currently 'native Americans', or 'American Indians'. In Canada the term 'First Nations' is commonly used, whereas in Alaska the preference is 'Alaskan Natives', to take into account the presence of Inuit, Yupik, and Aleut peoples.

Although many of the native tribes were friendly to the European explorers, the first group that Columbus met were the Arawaks on Haiti. Most of the 250,000 members of the tribe were violently enslaved; within a hundred years there were only 500 left, and within a few decades the entire culture was extinct. This was the most drastic example of European behaviour, however, over the next 400 years many other native cultures in the Americas were eradicated or altered beyond all recognition.

One of the biggest areas of conflict between the native American peoples and the European settlers concerned the interactions of man and nature. For many of the indigenous tribes, achieving harmony with the natural and spiritual worlds was of prime importance. This contrasted strongly with the approach the Europeans took, who viewed all they saw as an infinite resource for exploitation. For example, they believed there was a limitless supply of animals which could be killed for meat or to generate profits from fur trading. On top of this there were endless forests that could be cut down to provide timber or firewood. In some ways the belief that these resources were infinite is understandable - to the Europeans the sheer scale of the country must have been overwhelming. The concept that the natural bounty around them could not take sustained exploitation was outside their recognition.

As a result of seeing the level of abuse imposed on the environment by settlers, many native people found their actions to be unforgivable. On top of this, the European habit of claiming title to the ownership of lands that were historically those of native tribes was always going to end in conflict. The settlers generally considered the natives to be nomadic and therefore not interested in land ownership.

As more and more Europeans arrived, the pressure for living space grew. It was not long before tribes were being displaced, and this often ended in physical confrontation. The Indian Wars were met with absolute resolve by the white government, who put massive military forces into troubled areas to quell any uprisings. Often the authorities would make treaties to gain some form of peace - they would then ignore or nullify them, leaving the native Indians high and dry.

On January 31, 1876 the United States government finally ordered all native Indians to move from their homelands onto reservations or reserves. Many tribal factions refused to comply, and a series of battles ensued. In the end though, the native Indians were doomed to lose - they were outnumbered, outgunned and unable to unite against the enemy. One of the last, and in many ways most famous clashes occurred in 1890, when the U.S. cavalry massacred large numbers of Indian warriors, along with defenceless women and children at Wounded Knee, in South Dakota.

The story of the arrival of European settlers is not all bad, however. The Americas had been without horses since the end of the Ice Age, so when native Indians travelled across land, they did so on foot. Hunting bison, for instance, was a very difficult and unproductive affair unless you could keep up with them. Thus when the settlers brought horses with them, it was not long before the native Indians obtained their own. Some of these were undoubtedly stolen, others were the result of catching animals that had escaped and bred in the wild. Once they had their own horses, the culture of many tribes changed overnight. For a start they could chase bison over large distances, and having made their kills, they could transport the carcasses home with ease. This led to a level of prosperity many had never experienced before. Although it was a time of plenty, the native Indians understood the importance of remaining in balance with nature. As a result of this they only took what they could use. This was in stark contrast to the Europeans who would often kill huge numbers of bison just for their tongues, which were considered a delicacy. The remaining animal carcasses were just left to rot, something that was perceived as a crime against nature by native Indians.

After the Indian Wars were over, various methods were used to try and 'civilise' the native Indians. Some of these practices imposed untold misery on the unfortunate subjects. For over fifty years, from 1875 to 1928 children were forcibly taken from their tribal homes and sent to boarding schools. Here they were forbidden to speak their own languages and forced to speak English instead as well as follow European religions. Other indignities were enacted on native Indians as well - not only were they confined to their reservations, but in many cases were forced to undergo sterilisation or terminations against their wishes.

This catalogue of institutionalised abuse has left a massive residue of problems amongst large numbers of native Indians. These are the same kinds of problems that have also been experienced by other indigenous peoples around the world after their lands were settled by Europeans. At the heart of it all is poverty - this has often led to severe health problems. Sometimes these problems are due to alcoholism, and range from liver disorders to domestic violence. Dietary insufficiency has made obesity commonplace, which has led to very high rates of heart disease and diabetes.

Fortunately, the way that the American authorities have dealt with the native Indian peoples has, in recent times, changed beyond all recognition. These days there are organisations that provide everything from legal support to health advice. Some tribes have become extremely wealthy as a result of oil being found on their lands - others have built massive gambling empires. All in all, things are improving, and if all goes well the native Indians will once again prosper in America.

The most northerly region occupied by native American Indians covers the Arctic and Sub-Arctic; together these two zones form a vast area. The Arctic is comprised of the territories between the northern edge of the American continent and Greenland, and the Sub-Arctic is made up of the northern interior of Canada and the whole of Alaska. This includes the belt of semi-arctic land from the Rocky Mountains across to Hudson Bay.

The Arctic region remained in the grip of the last ice-age until about 4,000 years ago - consequently, it was uninhabitable by humans. As the last of the major glaciers

in this area melted, people slowly started settling there. There are three basic groups of native tribes in the region - these are the Inuit, the Yuit and the Aleut. The Inuit (often referred to as Eskimo) can be divided into six further groups - these are the Greenland Inuit (Kalaallit), the Labrador Inuit, the Central Inuit, the Banks Island Inuit, the Western Arctic Inuit (Inuvialuit), and the Alaskan Inuit. There are two groups of Yuits - the Alaskan and the Siberian Yuit, and only one group of Aleut.

The native tribes which chose to settle in the very north had to be extremely adept at

coping with such a cold climate. Like all human cultures, their two most basic needs to survive were food and shelter. In a place where there are no trees and little other vegetation, their resources were very limited. Farming is impossible in the far north - the Arctic winters are too harsh, and for six months of the year there is little or no daylight. In the sparse woodlands of the southernmost part of the region a certain amount of gathering could be done. At the right time of year berries could be collected, and when the ground was soft enough edible roots could be uncovered. Out on the ice, however, the choices were few and far between - with the exception of the occasional bird, the only significant source of food was from the sea. This included seals, walrus, and whales. On land there was more wildlife to hunt, with the caribou and moose being the mainstay.

Although these animals could provide plenty of food, the problem for the hunter was how to catch and kill their chosen prey. For most native tribes the preferred weapon was the bow and arrow, but for those who lived out on the ice there were no trees to make them from. The only source of timber to make them from in such places was driftwood, which is completely useless for this task. Bows are complicated structures, and can only be made

from certain kinds of wood. On top of this, the extreme cold makes most types of wood far too brittle to be used for bow making.

There were two main ways in which the natives got around this problem. The first was to obtain wood from the nearest mainland sources - in the far north the only species of tree that could cope with the low temperatures was birch. This is not the ideal material for bows - however, while it lacks strength, it is less brittle when cold than other woods. The second choice was to make their bows from antler horn. Once again, this material lacks strength, but can cope with the cold. No-one knows how long it took to develop the solution to this dilemma, but what they came up with really shows how clever these people were. They crafted the low-strength materials - birch or antler, to construct the actual body of the bow, which on its own would have been barely able to cast an arrow. To add power they reinforced the bow with complex backings and cables made from whale or caribou sinew. Although the resulting weapon would compare poorly with something like a longbow, it was capable of functioning at far lower temperatures. Such a bow would kill a seal at moderate ranges, and this facility made it possible to live out on the ice-sheets.

For those tribes that lived in suitable areas, trapping was a productive means of obtaining food. Many different kinds of small animals could be caught in this way - from mice to rabbits, all were a useful addition to the diet. When the ice on the rivers and lakes melted in spring, traps could also be used to catch fish. They could also be taken with spears and fish arrows, and all year long fishing with lines and hooks was undertaken.

With a source of food to hand, shelter was the other priority. The tribes that lived on land made tents from caribou skins, whereas those out on the ice constructed igloos from blocks of compacted snow. When a hunt was successful, every last piece of the animal was used. The meat was eaten - either on the spot or dried for later use. The skins were cured and used to make clothes, shoes, tents, and all manner of other essential items. The entrails were also used - in the case of caribou, partly-digested moss was considered a delicacy and eaten with relish. Certain parts of the gut were dried and used as binding materials for shoe-making, tent construction, attaching arrow heads or fletchings, and so on. Glue was made from boiling bones after the sinews had been carefully removed to be made into high strength cordage for all sorts of important uses.

The problem with hunting and gathering is that animals rarely stay in one place for long, and berries are only available at certain times of year. As a result the tribes had to be able to move in response to the changing seasons - this meant that their cultures developed into fully nomadic lifestyles. One of the characteristics of nomadic peoples is that the different tribal groups tend to develop different dialects - over periods of time these gradually become distinct languages. In the Arctic and Sub-Arctic region the main languages are derived from the Algonquian-Wakashan and the Nadene roots.

Aluet

The Aleuts are natives of West Alaska and the Aleutian Islands, which stretch for about 1,100 miles (1,800 km) south-westward from the Alaskan mainland. The Aleut call themselves 'unangan' which translates as 'the people'. Although they are most closely related to the Eskimo and Siberian peoples, their language and culture are different. Before the Europeans arrived on the scene, the Aleut lived in small villages in houses which were partly underground. They had a class system ruled by nobles, at the bottom of which were slaves. Shamans were an important part of the culture. The Aleut were hunter gatherers - at sea they would use lightweight boats covered with skins to take fish, seals, sea lion, and whales. On land they would search for eggs, roots and berries, and hunt for foxes, otters and birds. They traded a large proportion of the furs they obtained with Russian dealers, many of whom exploited them ruthlessly. Disease caught from incomers had a particularly drastic effect on their population, and it is estimated that today there are only a tenth of the numbers of Aleut that once existed.

ATHABASCAN

AMISKQUEW.

The Athabascan (also spelt 'Athapaskan') tribes probably arrived in the region as part of the final great migration wave over the last 1,000 years or so. The three tribes that were still in existence in the sub-Arctic region when the Europeans arrived have since all died out. The tribes who spoke Athabascan languages once lived throughout Alaska, Canada, Oregon, California, Arizona, New Mexico, Texas, and as far south as parts of Mexico. Today there are many tribes who still speak Athabascan languages - these include the Chipewyan, Kutchin, Carrier, Hupa, Navajo, and Apaches. In all this amounts to some 175,000 people in Canada and the United States, the majority of which are members of the Navajo tribe.

CHIPEWYAN

A-MIS-QUAM,
A WINNEBAGO BRAVE.

The Chipewyan tribe were once the largest group of Athabascan speaking people. They call themselves 'Dene', which translates as 'people'. The name Chipewyan comes from the Cree word meaning 'pointed skins'. They used to range over much of western Canada, along the fringes of the northern forests and well into the tundra areas between the Great Slave Lake and the Churchill River. They were nomadic hunter gatherers who lived in extended family groups and travelled after the herds of caribou along their seasonal migration routes. They suffered badly when exposed to European diseases, and smallpox in particular took a heavy toll on their numbers. Today there are some 10,000 living members of the Chipewyan tribe, and they are distributed across Alberta, Manitoba, Saskatchewan, and the Northwest Territories.

CREE

A NA CAM E GISH CA.
A CHIPPEWAY CHIEF.

The Cree are were the largest and most important tribe of native American Indians in Canada. They originally inhabited lands around Lakes Winnipeg and Manitoba and eastwards as far as Hudson Bay. The name 'Cree' comes from an Ojibwa word with an unknown meaning. They refer to themselves, however, as 'Eythinyuwuk', which simply translates as 'men'. They lived a hunter-gatherer existence, collecting fruit, berries, and roots, much of which would be pounded to remove moisture and then dried and put in storage for later use. They also went on hunting and fishing forays, with buffalo being especially sought after.

The Cree are closely related to the Ojibwa, and until the tribe was greatly weakened by smallpox in the late 1700's, they were one of the most powerful Native American Indian tribes. They had an alliance with the Assiniboin, some of whom joined up with members of one Cree faction and moved south to hunt buffalo - they established the plains Cree tribe. The Cree had long-running wars with the Sioux and Blackfeet tribes, amongst others. They were, however, generally friendly with both the English and French fur traders, who considered them to be good tempered, honest and generous.

Birchbark baskets

Calling a moose

Cree Boatwomen

Cree Fishing Camp

MÉTIS

AP·PA·NOO·SE
SAUKIE CHIEF.

The Metis are not a tribe, but a people. When the English, Scottish and French fur traders reached the Canadian north-west, it was not long before they started inter-breeding with women from the local native Indian settlements. These were mostly from the Cree or Ojibwa tribes. Their mixed-blood offspring eventually became so numerous that they evolved into a new and distinct Aboriginal nation - the Metis people. This began around the mid 1600's and continued to grow in size until the end of the 19th century. Since they had roots in both the native and European cultures, they were able to communicate well with both factions. As a result of this, many established what became very successful companies, transporting provisions the long distances from the towns and ports to the furthest outposts where they were traded for furs. One of their most popular commodities was buffalo meat. A lot of Metis villages were built around the places where the fur trade was practised, and many of these have since grown into large towns.

ESKIMO

The term Eskimo (sometimes spelt ' Esquimaux') refers to a number of different native groups of the Arctic region between the Chukchi Peninsula in north eastern Siberia, across the Bering Straits and over as far west as Greenland. The groups from Canada and Greenland prefer to be referred to as Inuit (which translates as 'The People'), although many of the native people of Alaska and Siberia do not use the name. There are many distinct Eskimo dialects used by the many groups across the region, however, they all have very similar cultures. No-one knows when the Eskimo peoples first crossed into the Americas from north east Asia, but it is believed that they were part of the last major migration wave which occurred over the past 5,000 years. They are racially distinct from the native American Indians, their closest relatives being the Mongolians. The groups that live in the most northerly areas hunt whales and seals, whereas those from the Pacific coast mostly fish for salmon, and those from mainland Canada generally hunt caribou. The population of the Eskimo peoples was around 50,000 when they experienced their first contact with Europeans - today the number is about the same.

A typical Hoonah squaw

Alaska Siwash motherhood

Nash Harbor, Nunivak

Baninaguh, Nunivak

Bark dishes, Kobuk

Baskets, Nunivak

Chilkat - image on Chief's grave

Chilkat Indians in dancing costumes, Alaska

Chilkat woman weaving blanket, Alaska

Dishes, Nunivak

Eskimos in kayaks, Noatak, Alaska

Fish-drying racks, Nunivak

Herring racks, Nunivak

Indian dancers at Potlatch, Chilkat, Alaska

Jukuk, Nunivak

Kaiak frame, Nunivak

Looking to sea, King Island

Maskette, Nunivak

Noatak child

Noatak home

Nunivak youth

On Kotzebue Sound

Selawik girl

Start of whale hunt, Cape Prince of Wales

Tahopik, Diomede

The beluga, Kotzebue

The bow-drill, King Island

The ivory carver, Nunivak

The umiak, Kotzebue

Waterproof parkas, Nunivak

Northwest Coast and California

Northwest Coast

The North-western coastal region runs for more than 2,000 miles along the edge of the Pacific Ocean from Alaska to California. It is around 150 miles deep, and also includes western British Columbia, Washington and Oregon. There are offshore islands which fall into this culture area as well - these stretch from near Yakutat Bay in the

north, to Washington Strait in the south. The largest of these are Vancouver Island, the Queen Charlotte Islands and the Alexander Archipelago. Along the northern shores of the region there are many sheltered inlets which act as excellent natural harbours. The region includes two major mountain ranges - these are the Cascades, which are situated in the United States, and the Coast Range in Canada.

The temperate environment is beneficial towards human existence, although rather wet. There is a very high annual rainfall, which encourages the large numbers of trees which cover most of the area to grow prolifically. The first native Indians arrived on the north-west coast around 12,000 years ago. They found that the area was rich in land animals as well as fish - on top of this there were lots of seed bearing plants, nuts, berries and other wild fruits to collect.

The sea provided a bountiful harvest - fish included salmon, halibut, cod and

flounder, while marine mammals included dolphins, whales, otters, seals, and sea-lions. Fish were not only seen as food - when their bones were boiled up, they also provided powerful glues. Almost all the animals that were hunted yielded meat as well as skins and other useful commodities. The land mammals that were on the menu included deer, elk, bears, and mountain goats.

The fact that the sea provided a rich harvest encouraged the native tribes people to become excellent inshore mariners. They travelled great distances using canoes and kayaks, but had to be very skilled in their use because the tides along the coast are amongst the highest in the world. This produces incredibly strong currents, which can easily overwhelm a novice.

The tribes had such a plethora of foods to choose from that they did very little farming - except that is, for growing tobacco. The ease of collecting food meant there was plenty of time left over for cultural activities, and they developed complex societal systems. Smoking was a part of many social and ceremonial functions, and tobacco was therefore an important crop.

Many large settlements were established along the coast close to the best fishing grounds. These were generally composed of wooden houses which each contained an extended family. The houses themselves were made of substantial frames made from tree trunks, which were then planked with wide cedar boards.

Ceremonies and rituals were an important part of community life, and most of them involved dressing up in costumes. Neighbouring villages often participated in significant events - the most important of which was a special feast called a potlatch. At these ceremonies affluent individuals gave away many of their possessions - this helped them establish their ranking within the tribe - the higher their rank, the more they gave away. These gatherings helped to bond people and minimise the risk of friction between local tribes.

The amount of time these people had on their hands can also be seen in their artwork. They developed excellent wood working skills, and these were put to good use in creating distinctive wood carvings. Their high carpentry standards were also demonstrated in the construction of cedar planked canoes and carved dugouts. These days the best known wooden native artefacts are probably totem poles - these were carved structures adorned with all sorts of animal decoration that were erected in the permanent winter settlements in front of each building. The actual animals depicted on the totem poles were carefully chosen by the shamans, as they had particular significance to the tribe.

The North-western natives also made many ceremonial art objects, especially masks. More everyday items were also crafted to high standards, these include baskets made from reeds, and woven textiles which were used to make blankets and clothes. These were often traded amongst the tribes of the region. Trade - which was popular, was helped by a monetary system based on seashells.

There were so many different tribes in the region that a large number of different languages existed alongside one another. In the north, the Na-Dene language family was the most widespread, and the Wakashan and Penutian variants predominated in the central areas.

Although the European settlers first arrived on the East coast at the end of the 1400's, it took them nearly 300 years to make their way across the vast continent of America. Consequently, the native Indian cultures which had been in this region for some 12,000 years, were not significantly disrupted by settlers until comparatively recently - some 260 years ago. Sadly, many of the tribes did not survive the exposure to new diseases, or the strange and often hostile ways of the new incomers.

CALIFORNIA

The native American Indian region known as the California culture area covers most of the United States between the Northwest coastal region and Mexico. It includes the southernmost parts of Oregon, most of the state of California, and reaches down to the Baja peninsula in Mexico. The eastern borders are formed by the Sierra Nevada Mountains and the Gulf of California, while the western limits are marked by the Pacific Ocean. There is a lot of overlap between the California culture area and those of the Great Basin and South-western areas, and also many influences from the Northwest and Great Plateau cultures.

The environment in the California culture area varies tremendously depending on the location. There are many mountains and a lot of high ground in the region, with two mountain ranges - the Coast Range and the Sierra Nevadas stretching from north down towards Mexico. In the south it is hot and arid, and desert conditions predominate. There are extensive mountain deserts as well, and while these are beautiful places, they are harsh places to try and survive in. There are very few rivers, and those that do flow, often only do so in the winter months.

In the more northerly areas there is a high annual rainfall, and temperatures can fall much lower than in the southern areas. There are many redwood forests, and some of the tallest trees in the world are to be found in places like the Yosemite and Sequoia national parks. As a result of the amount of rain that falls there are lots of rivers that start out high up in the hills and gradually work their way down until they eventually reach the Pacific Ocean. There were good natural resources to be found in the region - the rivers and sea offered excellent fishing, and the forests provided the opportunity to hunt all manner of animals, from rabbits to bear, lynx, mountain lion and deer.

The tribes in the California culture area varied as much as the terrain - most, however, were centred around permanent villages composed of extended families. These were presided over by a head man, who organised or advised on everything from ceremonial functions to hunting and fishing expeditions.

ACHOMAWI (FROM ADZÚMA, OR ACHÓMA, 'RIVER').

ASSEOLA.
A SEMINOLE LEADER.

The Achomawi (also spelt Achumawi) who were also known as the Pit River Indians, were a group of native Indians that originally inhabited lands in the region of the Pit River in north-east California. The river itself was named by early white settlers because of the number of pitfall traps along the trails in the area - these were used by the local Indians to catch deer. These were very common in the forests of the region, and provided an excellent supply of venison as well as skins, sinew and many other products. Deerskin was used for making many different clothing items, including leggings, moccasins, belts, skirts, shirts, caps, and so on. Religion played a key part in the tribe's culture, the central figures of which were shamans - many of whom were women.

Achomawi basket maker

Achomawi man

Achomawi woman and child

Achomawi hut

NUXALK OR BELLA COOL

CA-TA-HE-CAS-CA BLACK HOOF
PRINCIPAL CHIEF OF THE SHAWANOES

The Nuxalk - who were also known as the Bella Coola, were an ancient group of tribes that inhabited large tracts of land in the region of the central Pacific Coast. They were in the area living among the mountains and fjords for the best part of ten thousand years before the European settlers arrived. Their territories were composed of temperate rainforests, and measured something in the order of 16,000 km_. As with so many other native peoples, they have had all this taken from them by the United States government. The matter is still being disputed, and in 1995 many tribal members raised a protest where they blockaded logging operations to try and force the authorities to deal with their concerns. These include putting a stop to logging, since the forests cannot sustain the demands being made on them for timber. They also want fishing to be restricted for similar reasons. The protestors were promptly arrested, and three of the chiefs were imprisoned for four weeks. These days there are about 3,000 living members of the Nuxalk, about 900 of whom live on the seven reserves they were assigned in the Bella Coola valley area.

Cahuilla

CHIPPEWAY SQUAW & CHILD

The Cahuilla were a group of native Indians who inhabited their lands for at least 2,000 years. These covered the Borrego to Riverside area and measured around 2,400 square miles in total. There were three main divisions - these were the Mountain, Desert and Pass Cahuillas. Some groups had particular names, such as the Agua Caliente, Morongo, Los Coyotes, Torres-Martinez, Cabazon and Santa Rosa Indians. The men were hunters who used a variety of weapons, from bows and arrows to throwing sticks and clubs. They also used various kinds of traps to catch their prey which ranged from small animals such as rabbit, through to bighorn sheep, deer and antelope. The women were gatherers who collected a wide selection of wild produce such as acorns, cactus fruits, grass seeds, mesquite beans, pine nuts and others. Some of these were eaten immediately or stored away for use during periods of drought or cold weather. Others, however, had medicinal or utilitarian uses. The Cahuilla were similar to many of the other native Indian peoples of the region in that they were skilled at making pottery and weaving baskets. Their remote desert location meant that they escaped many of the problems associated with European settlers arriving in the area. They were hit badly by imported diseases though - it is thought that their population was once as large as 10,000, but after a smallpox epidemic hit them in 1862, only 2,500 or so survived. There are now 10 reservations in Southern California, and some of the tribe earn an income from tourism.

Cahuilla child

A man of Palm Springs--Cahuilla

Cahuilla house in the desert, California

Fiesta camp (Cahuilla)

Numero - Desert Cahuilla

Marcos - Palm Canyon

A Desert Cahuilla woman

The Harvest - Desert Cahuilla

Under the palms - Cahuilla

Chehalis or Upper Kwaiailk

The Chehalis peoples originally occupied large homelands within the Chehalis River Watershed - these covered an area which reached from the foothills of the Cascade Mountains across to the Pacific Ocean in Southwest Washington. When it was first used, the name 'Chehalis' actually referred to a group of several different Salishan tribes who lived in the region. Their homes, which were constructed from cedar planks, were situated along the larger rivers and waterways. They used the rivers and sea to provide their main sources of food - these included salmon, eels, clams and crayfish. In 1860 they were moved onto a local reservation which lies across the borders of Thurston and Grays Harbour Counties. It measures just over 4,200 acres. Although there are now more than 650 living members of the Chehalis Tribe, in 1910 their numbers dropped below 150.

CHIMAKUM AND QUILLIUTE

CHITTEE YOHOLO

The Chimakuan were formerly a group of native Indians from the coastal area of Washington. By the time European settlers arrived, however, there were only two tribes left - the Quileute, who still survive, and an eastern tribe called the Chimakum, who are thought to have been wiped out through warfare with other tribes. It is believed that the tribes were once much larger, and that they were driven from their homelands by the Clallani and Makah tribes. Although the Chimakuan were mostly friendly towards white settlers, they had a powerful reputation amongst other native tribes for their abilities as warriors. They were also very accomplished sailors, and derived much of their food by whaling from small boats. The Chimakum still survived into the late 1890s, but they appear to have all since disappeared.

Chimakum female

Chimakum female

Quilliute girl

Silto - Quilliute

CINOOKAN TRIBES

CHON-MON-I-CASE
AN OTTO HALF CHIEF

The Chinook were a tribe of native Indians whose homelands were situated along the lower Columbian River. This waterside location meant that they became expert sailors and fishermen. When the salmon were running in their thousands as part of their spawning cycle, the Chinook were able to catch so many fish that they had more than they could ever need themselves. As a result they built up a large trading network which reached as far as tribes that lived thousands of miles away. They also exchanged other things too - these included seashells, which some tribes used as currency, and also canoes as well as slaves. They came into conflict with European traders, and their population started to fall. In the end they were forced off their lands and placed on reservations.

Chinook woman

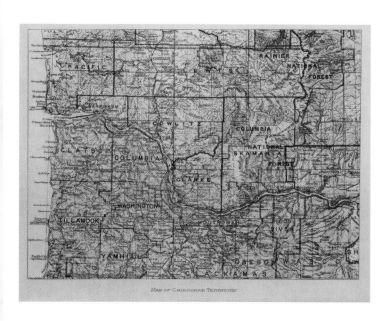

Map of chinook territory

On the beach - Chinook

HAIDA

SHOND CA PE
AN OTTOE CHIEF

The Haida were native Indians who lived off the mainland on the Queen Charlotte Islands, off the coast of British Columbia, and on the southern end of the Prince of Wales Island, which is off the coast of Alaska. Their settlements were composed of large houses that were built from wide cedar planks. Their culture was that of hunters - they caught salmon from the shores and hunted for seals, walrus and other sea mammals from their sturdy dugout canoes. Their tribes were split into two groups - these were called the Eagle and Raven clans. In the days before the white settlers arrived, the Haida numbered around 8,000, but after a series of disease epidemics struck the area - particularly smallpox, this was reduced to around 2,000 in the late 1870s. Many of the surviving members of the tribe are employed in fishing and in canning.

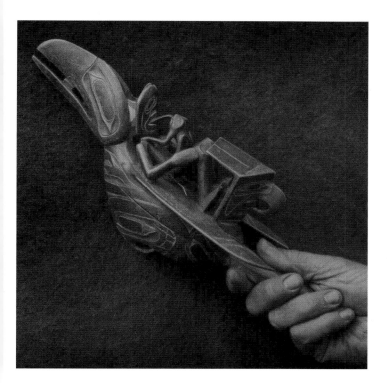

A Haida shaman's rattle

A woman of Kiusta (Haida)

Chilikat blanket, the Haida ceremonial robe

Hahlkaiyans, of Massett (Haida)

Haida canoe

Haida chief's tomb at Yan

Haida of Massett

Haida slate carvings

Haida slate carving

Raven chief of Skidegate (Haida)

Shaman's rattle (Haida)

Kitkun, of Massett (Haida)

Slate carvings representing a Haida shaman

Stlina, of Massett (Haida)

HOOPA

DAVID VANN.

The Hoopa (also spelt 'Hupa') tribe formerly occupied lands in the region of the Trinity River between Hoopa valley and the Klamath River in north-west California. They were hunters and gatherers, and were the most southerly based of the native Indians of the north-west culture area. They travelled extensively along the waterways of the region in dugout canoes looking for places to fish for salmon or to collect wild produce. One of their mainstays was acorns, which they made into a kind of bread. Their settlements contained houses made from wide cedar planks - these had no windows and only a small circular opening as a door. The United States government assigned their lands as a reservation in 1864, where they are still located.

Costume of the obsidian-bearer (Hupa)

Dancer with black deer effigy (Hupa)

Fish-weir across Trinity River - Hupa

Fishing from canoe - Hupa

Hupa basket and purses

Hupa baskets

Hupa fisherman

Hupa jumping dance costume

Hupa mother and child

Hupa purses and money

Hupa sweat-house

Hupa trout-trap

Hupa woman in primitive costume

Hupa woman

Hupa woman's dress

Principal female shaman of the Hupa

Smoky day at the Sugar Bowl - Hupa

Sticks used in Hupa guessing game

KAROK

ELS-KWAL-SEA-WAW,
The Open Door

The Karok (also spelt Karuk) originally inhabited lands on the middle course of the Klamath River, between the Trinity River and the mouth of Bluff Creek where they had around 36 settlements. They were one of the first peoples to populate the area, some 10,000 years ago. The name 'Karok' translates as 'upstream'. They were a sedentary hunter gatherer tribe whose culture was based around salmon fishing, however, since redwood trees did not grow on their territories they could not make their own dugout canoes. To get around this they traded with the Yurok instead. The Karok suffered badly when gold was discovered on their homelands - the rush of ruthless miners into the region soon brought conflict and tragedy on both sides. In 1875, the gold seekers killed 75 Karok people, which caused them to move away until the fever for treasure died down. These days the tribe numbers around 2,000 people.

Karok baskets

Karok woman

Old Bob

KATO/CAHTU

ESH-TAH-HUM-LEAH
or the Sleepy Eye

The Kato or Cahto were the southernmost Athapaskans on the Pacific Coast, and formerly inhabited lands on the upper drainage of the south fork of the Eel River where they had 15 to 20 settlements. They were a sedentary hunter gatherer tribe who, like the Karok and other tribes in the area suffered badly from the influx of gold prospectors in 1850. They also had violent conflicts with the Yuki tribe - these problems conspired to reduce their population from about 500 in 1850 to less than 60 in 1910. These days their numbers have risen to 600 or so, most of whom now live on the Laytonville Reservation.

A Kato matron

A Kato woman

Tachahaqachile (Kato)

Northwest Coast and California

Kwakuitl (Kwakwala)

The Kwakiutl were a native Indian people who inhabited north Vancouver Island and most of the coastline of British Columbia, Canada. They were very skilled woodworkers, and became well known for their excellent carvings. These decorative techniques were used to decorate totem poles, the gable ends of houses, mortuary posts, masks and for many other purposes. The Kwakiutl's culture was typical of the Pacific north-west area, and included most of the rituals common in the region. The best known of these was the Potlatch ceremony, where valued items were distributed among the tribe.

A housefront (Awaitlala)

A Kwakiutl canoe

A Kwaustums village

A Nakoaktok mawihl

A Tluwulahu mask (Tswatenok)

A Tsawatenok house-front

A Tsunukwa at Kwaustums

An incident of the winter dance (Nakoaktok)

At Memkumlis

Bridal group

Carved posts at Alert Bay

Dancing to restore an eclipsed moon - Qagyuhl

Group of winter dancers - Qagyuhl

Hamasaka in Tlu'wulahu costume

Hamatsa (Qagyuhl)

In Kwakiutl waters

Kekuhtlala (Koeksotenok)

Komuqi (Qagyuhl)

Koskimo house-post

Kotsuis and Hohhuq - Nakoaktok

Kwakiutl house-frame

Lagyus (Tsawatenok)

Masked dancers - Qagyuhl

Naemahlpunkuma (Hahuamis)

Nakoaktok chief and copper

Nakoaktok chief's daughter

Nane (Qagyuhl)

Nimkish village at Alert Bay

Nultsi (Lekwiltok)

Nunalalahl (Qagyuhl)

Painting a hat - Nakoaktok

Pgwis (Qagyuhl)

NORTHWEST COAST AND CALIFORNIA

Qagyuhl village at Fort Rupert

Qunhulahl (Qagyuhl)

Sisiutl (Qagyuhl)

Tawihyilahl (Qagyuhl)

Tenaktak canoes

Tenaktak crest posts, Harbledown Island

Northwest Coast and California

Tenaktak house, Harbledown Island

The octopus catcher (Qagyuhl)

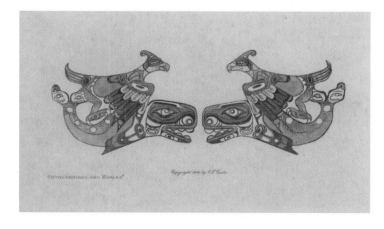

Thunderbirds and whales

MAIDU

TOKE-LULITE-HAJO

The Maidu were a widespread group that formerly occupied lands that ranged from Nevada to the foothills of the Sacramento Valley. In all there were about 74 different settlements, the most southern group - the Nishinam, was in the Bear River Valley, and the most northern group was located south of Mount Lassen. The tribe were hunter gatherers - the area was so rich in wild foodstuffs that they never needed to do any farming. Acorns were a staple part of their diet - they were collected and stored in large quantities for later use. Game animals were also plentiful in the woods and forests, and the rivers were full of fish. The Maidu settlements were usually situated such that the trails leading up to them could be watched for approaching strangers. The permanent houses that were used in cold weather were large semi-subterranean circular affairs. These were built from a pole framework with a thick covering of mud which made them very warm; each building would house several families. In the warmer months they would live in more temporary structures made of branches and then covered with brush.

A Maidu boy

A Maidu man

A Maidu woman

Otila (Maidu)

MIWOK ('MAN')

The Miwok were native Indians who were said to be the largest peoples in California. They were split into three distinct culture groups - the Valley Miwok occupied the western slope of the Sierra Nevadas from the Sacramento - San Joaquin delta and Cosumnes River south to the Fresno River. The lands of the Coast Miwok stretched from the Golden Gate north to Duncan's Point, and then east as far as Sonoma Creek. The Lake Miwok inhabited an area in the basin of Clear Lake. They were hunter gatherers who were thriving until the arrival of white settlers, when diseases reduced their numbers considerably. They were almost wiped out when this was compounded by violent conflicts with Mexican and American gold rush settlers.

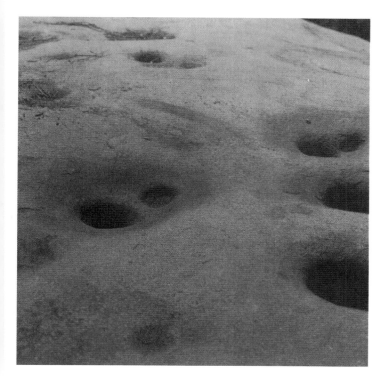

A boulder milling-stone - Miwok

A southern Miwok - Profile

A southern Miwok woman

Fisherman - Southern Miwok

Fishing-pool - Southern Miwok

Miwok head-man

miwok home yosemite ca

miwok platforms yosemite ca

miwok women pose yosemite ca

miwok yosemite ca

moqui hairdresser

On the Merced - Southern Miwok

Sifting basket (Southern Miwok)

Southern Miwok

NOOTKA (NOO-CHAH-NULTH)

The Nootka are a small group of native Indians who live on the western shore of Vancouver Island, British Columbia. In the nineteenth century they were typical of the north-west coast culture, and were proficient fishermen who also hunted seals, whales and sea otters. The principle fish species they caught were halibut, cod and salmon. When gathering wild produce they collected various berries, roots and nuts. Although their carving and painting skills were not a match for some of those of other tribes in the region, they were expert basket weavers. Before white settlers arrived they numbered around 6,000, however, this figure dropped to just over 2,000 at the beginning of the twentieth century. Their population has since recovered to more or less the pre-settler level.

A Nootka woman

A Nootka

A raven totem at Yan

At Nootka

NORTHWEST COAST AND CALIFORNIA

Dancing Mask (Nootka)

Haiyahl - Nootka

Makah basketry

Nootka man

Nootka man

Nootka method of spearing

Nootka woman wearing cedar-bark blanket

NORTHWEST COAST AND CALIFORNIA

Oldest man of Nootka

On the shores at Nootka

Sepulture in a post at Yan

Shores of Nootka Sound

The bear costume (Nootka)

The lake at Nootka

The shores of the Nootka

Totem at Yan, representing a Caucasian

Totems at Kung

Totems at Yan.

POMO

HOO-WAN-NE-KA.
A WINNEBAGO CHIEF.

The Pomo were a people who lived along the Northern California coast in parts of Sonoma, Lake, Mendocino, Colusa, and Glenn Counties; the name 'Pomo' means 'people' in their own dialect.

They were sedentary hunter gatherers who were generally peaceful both to other tribes and to white settlers. Their basketry skills were possibly the best of all the tribes in North America, and they particularly liked using decorative things like feathers to adorn their personal belongings. They suffered very badly from problems generated by white missionaries, as well as from those caused by gold rush settlers. Their population currently numbers around 800, and many of them live on the Round Valley Reservation.

A Pomo camp

Aged Pomo woman

Basket used in puberty rites (Pomo)

Canoe of tules - Pomo

Coast Pomo bridal costume

Coast Pomo girl

Coast Pomo woman

Conception rock near Ukiah (Pomo)

Cooking acorns - Lake Pomo

Kohnono (Pomo)

Mixed-blood Coast Pomo

Old Ukiah - Pomo

Pomo baskets and magnesite beads

Pomo baskets, mortar, and pestle

Pomo baskets

Pomo dance costume

Pomo girl

Pomo mother and child

SALISHAN TRIBES OF COAST

JACK-O-PA

The Coastal Salish occupied lands along the Pacific coast of British Columbia, from the Strait of Georgia down through Puget Sound in Washington State and as far south as the Siletz River in Oregon. The Bella Coola were situated further north along the Burke Channel in British Columbia. The area around the mouth of the Columbia River was, however, inhabited by the Chinook, who were not part of the group. Most of the coastal Salish dwellings were made of wide planks with heavy beams, and contained several families, each with their own fireplace. Catching fish from canoes or with nets from the shore where they also collected shellfish were mainstay occupations for most of these people. The tribes in this region were not exposed to significant numbers of settlers until much later than most other tribes across America. This was because the ownership of the area was being argued over by the United States and Great Britain. In 1909 there were approximately 8,500 Salish living along the coasts of the United States and Canada.

SHOSHONE (SOUTHERN CALIFORNIA)

JOHN RIDGE.
A CHEROKEE.

It is believed that the tribes that made up the coastal Shoshone group migrated to the Pacific coast from the Great Basin culture area. They occupied lands along the coast in parts of southern California where they had a culture which featured strong religious beliefs based around mysticism.

The tribes that comprised this group included the Serrano, Gabrieleño, Agua Caliente, Juaneño, Kawia, and Luiseño. These tribes all had similar methods of obtaining food, with their diets being made up of a wide variety of wild produce including creatures they hunted such as fish, sea lions, deer and various small game animals. They also collected seeds, acorns, pine nuts, berries and fruit.

SILETZ

JOHN ROSS.
A CHEROKEE CHIEF.

The Siletz tribe originally occupied lands in Lincoln County which is in north-western Oregon. Their ancestors had been in the coastal region for thousands of years, in what are now the Tillamook, Lincoln, and Lane Counties. The Siletz were the southernmost of the Salish tribes of the Pacific Coast, but were forced to move onto a reservation in 1855. The Siletz name was later used to refer to a confederation which was formed from 27 different tribal bands. These tribes came from a region which stretched from Northern California to south-west Washington state. They were all moved to the Siletz Reservation in Oregon in 1851. When gold was discovered in the area many thousands of white miners descended in the hope that they would make themselves a fortune. Many of them were very aggressive towards the native Indians. The reservation was split in two when the government came under pressure to build a railroad through the area. Further reservation lands were lost to settlers, and the authorities managed to take most of the rest by removing their official tribal recognition. After much protest, this was finally reinstated in 1977 with the Siletz Restoration Act.

TLINGIT

JTUHO-TCLTINNTOSNE

The Tlingit (also spelt Tlinget, Tlinkit, and Tlinket) formerly occupied homelands along the coast of southern Alaska and on the many islands off the coast. There were 14 different bands within the tribe, and although they were very proficient fishermen, they were also successful traders. They often travelled into the inland areas of Alaska and transported produce from the native Indians back to the coast. They then exchanged them with the white traders who usually only operated in places accessible by boat. In the late 1700s the Russians built a fort on their lands, which the Tlingit objected to. Eventually they managed to force the Russians to leave, however, when they returned there was a violent battle and many tribal members were killed. This trouble continued for many years. Nowadays the Tlingit live on reservations in British Columbia and Alaska.

TOLOWA

JULOEE-MATCHA.
A SEMINOLE CHIEF.

Their ancestors arrived in the area from Canada sometime after 1000 AD, and since then the tribe obtained most of their food by fishing. When the white settlers and miners came to the area they brought many virulent diseases with them, and the 1850s in particular were a decade of epidemics of measles and cholera. This reduced their numbers considerably, and today only about 200 survivors remain - most of them are located on the Elk Valley and Smith River Rancherias.

A Tolowa

Elk Horn Spoons

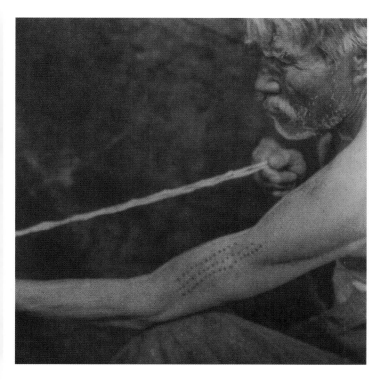

Measuring Shell Money

Tolowa Dancing Headdress

Tolowa Man

Tolowa Tatooing

Tolowa Woman in Primitive Dress

Tsimshian

KAI-POL-E-QUAR.

The Tsimshian (also spelt 'Chimmesyan') occupied lands along the coast of British Columbia, and north into Alaska. Their culture was typical of the north-west Coast area - they used canoes to fish for cod and halibut at sea, where they also hunted for seals and sea lions. They also caught large numbers of salmon as they moved upstream to spawn each spring, and hunted for bears, mountain goats, and deer. These days the Tsimshian live in British Columbia and Alaska, where they still do a lot of fishing, but they also generate incomes from forestry. In all there are about 12,000 tribal members who live in Canada and the United States.

TUTUTNI

KA.NA.PI.MA.
AN OTTAWA CHIEF.

The Tututni originally occupied lands along the Illinois and lower Rogue rivers in south-western Oregon, and on the coast either side of its mouth; they were often also referred to as the 'Coast Rogues'. Their first contact with European explorers happened in the early 1790s, and traders soon followed behind. They brought with them many diseases which reduced their population to around 1,300 in the early 1850s. At this time there were 8 groups living on the coast and 3 along the banks of the Rogue river. In 1857 they were forcibly removed to the Siletz Reservation as prisoners of war.

WAILAKI (WINTUN: 'NORTHERN LANGUAGE')

The Wailaki were a native Indian people that originally lived on the Eel River as far as the border of Yuki territory at the Big Bend; they also lived along several tributaries. Their culture was typical of coastal hunter gatherers, with fishing providing the mainstay of their food supplies. They did not use canoes to do this, but instead used spears and nets. The women collected many kinds of wild produce, including roots, seeds, nuts, fruit and berries, and the men hunted deer and other game animals. Their ancestors arrived on the Pacific Coast from Canada soon after the turn of the first millennium. They soon came into conflict with white settlers, and were forced to move to the Round valley Reservation where some of the tribe still live.

A Wailaki Man

A Wailaki Woman

Mitat - Wailaki

WASHOE

KEE-SHES-WA,

The Washoe (also spelt Washo) originally occupied lands in the region around the Washoe and Tahoe lakes in western Nevada and eastern California. Before this they lived further east, but conflicts with the Northern Paiute forced them to move westwards. They were a semi-sedentary hunter gatherer culture who managed to avoid contact with white incomers for a long time. This helped them avoid the diseases which decimated so many other native tribes. They did, however, lose most of their lands to white settlement. These days the surviving Washoe members live on reservations in California and Nevada.

A Washo Gem

Daitoli, Washo Basket Maker

Moder Designs on Washo Basket Making

Scraping a Deerskin (Washo)

Washo Baskets

Washo Cradle Baskets

Washo House

Washo Woman

WILLAPA

KEE-SHES-WAA.
A FOX WARRIOR

The Willapa were one of a small group of tribes in the Chinookian group of native Indian peoples, and their homelands had the most northern location of these. They were situated along the Willapa River and around the Willapa Bay area. To their south were the Chinook tribe, who, in 1970, had a population of 609 surviving members. The Chinookian tribes were skilled fishermen who took advantage of the natural abundance of salmon during the spawning run every spring. They were also active gatherers who dug for roots and collected acorns, berries and fruit. The men hunted for deer, elk and game birds. The Willapa tribe are now extinct, although quite when this occurred is not clear.

WINTUN

The Wintun (who were also known as the 'Wintu') occupied homelands on the west side of the Sacramento Valley - this was bordered in the north by Mount Shasta. They were hunter gatherers who were very proficient fishermen - their large catches of salmon were largely dried and stored. They also collected lots of wild produce, including many kinds of roots, berries, pine nuts, and acorns. The tribe suffered terribly from the attempted genocide imposed on them when the area was under Mexican rule. On top of this their numbers were markedly reduced by virulent diseases caught from the gold rush settlers and miners. In recent times their numbers have recovered to a certain extent, and these days the tribal population is around 3,200

WIYOT

KISH-KALL-WA
Shawnee Chief.

The Wiyot tribe formerly occupied homelands on Humbolt Bay and on the lower Eel and the Mad Rivers. They were sedentary coastal hunter gatherers who were primarily fishermen, taking most of the common species including cod and salmon. They were largely unaffected by the arrival of Europeans until the gold rush brought thousands of greedy prospectors and settlers to the area in 1850. It was not long before violent conflicts ensued, especially when a find was made on their territory at a place that became known as Gold Bluffs. There were many large-scale atrocities committed against tribal members in the years that followed, but things got much worse when up to a hundred women and children were massacred by a militia gang. In 1908, the Wiyot peoples established the Table Bluff Rancheria, in Loleta where about 250 of them still live today. The tribe lost its official status in 1953, but things started to improve when their rancheria received government recognition in 1981.

YOKUTS - MARIPOSAN FAMILY

The Yokuts peoples were originally located along the whole length of the San Joaquin valley, in central California, from the San Joaquin River up to the foothills of the Tehachapi mountains and along the edge of the Sierra Nevadas. They were part of a language group known as the 'Mariposan family' - mariposa being the Spanish word for butterfly. The group was composed of up to 50 different tribes, and most of them experienced terrible depredations when the area was under Mexican rule. This was compounded by the white settlers and miners who did their best to wipe the all the tribes in the area out. Their settlements often had a long communal house with separate entrances for each family. The women were skilled basket weavers, and the men used the bow and arrow to hunt for game animals. It is thought that there are currently around 2,500 members of the Yokuts peoples alive today.

A Chukchansi Yokuts woman

A Chukchansi Yokuts woman

A Yauelmani Yokuts

Among the tules (Yokuts)

Animal designs in Yokuts basketry

Art as old as the tree - southern Yokuts

Chukchansi Yokut Woman

Chukchansi Yokut Man

Cradle-basket - Chukchantsi Yokuts

Jack Rowan (Chukchansi Yokuts)

Rattlesnake design in Yokuts basketry

Rattlesnake design in Yokuts basketry

Northwest Coast and California

The hunting basket

Washo Basketry

Yauelmani Yokuts

Yokuts basketry designs

YUKIAN FAMILY

KISH-KE-KOSH

The Yuki originally occupied lands above the north fork of the Eel River - there is some archaeological evidence that they were the first native peoples to inhabit California. They were a group of sedentary hunter gatherers who were divided into several separate tribes. It is said that they were very warlike - indeed, their name means 'enemy' in the Wintun language, because of the fact that they often had violent conflicts with neighbouring tribes. When white settlers arrived in the region the Yuki's aggressive habits led to them being almost completely exterminated. Most of the survivors were moved to the Round River Reservation in 1864. These days there are only about 100 living Yuki members.

NORTHWEST COAST AND CALIFORNIA

A Yuki Woman

Modern Yuki Cabin

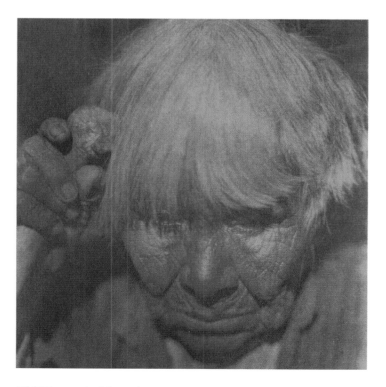

Old Woman in Mourning

YUROK

The Yurok originally inhabited lands in the valley of the lower Klamath River and the neighbouring coastal areas. The earliest known Yurok archaeological remains have been dated to around 1300 AD. They were sedentary coastal hunter gatherers who obtained most of their food by collecting acorns and by fishing for salmon. They used tusk shells as currency, and as a tribe they were relatively successful until the arrival of white settlers and miners with whom they had many conflicts. Their numbers were reduced by disease epidemics brought to the area by the newcomers, and in 1855 the authorities assigned them a reservation at which time their population numbered around 2,500. This fell to less than 500 in the 1930s, but has since risen to around 2,300. Most of the surviving Yurok members live on the Elk Valley and Trinidad Rancherias and the Yurok Reservation.

A Yurok cemetery

An ancient Yurok

Bob Peters, Trinidad Yurok

Fishing for smelt in the surf (Trinidad Yurok)

Old sweat-house walls at Orleans bar (Karok)

Quiet waters - Yurok

Sam Ewing - Yurok

Smelt fisher - Trinidad Yurok

The mush-basket (Karok)

Weitchpec George (Yurok)

A Clayoquot maiden

A Clayoquot woman

Berry-picker - Clayoquot

Clayoquot girl

Clayoquot man

Clayoquot woman in cedar-bark hat

Costume of a woman shaman (Clayoquot)

Fish spearing - Clayoquot

Into the shadow - Clayoquot

On Clayoquot Sound

Whale ceremonial - Clayoquot

Whaler - Clayoquot

A Cowichan mask

Carved figure (Cowichan)

Cowichan canoes

Cowichan girl

Cowichan houseframe

Cowichan River

Cowichan warrior

Cowichan woman

Gathering tules (Cowichan)

Goathair blanket (Cowichan)

Henipsum village (Cowichan)

Looking up Cowichan River

Masked dancer (Cowichan)

Masked dancer (Cowichan)

Qamutsun village (Cowichan)

Spearing salmon - Cowichan

Tule gatherer - Cowichan

Warrior's feather head-dress (Cowichan)

Warrior's scalp head-dress

A Klamath costume

A Klamath man

A Klamath woman

A Klamath man

Chief - Klamath

Gathering wokas - Klamath

Grinding wokas (Klamath)

In the forest - Klamath

Klamath child

Klamath hunter

Klamath warrior's headdress

Klamath woman

Old Klamath woman

Wife of Modoc Henry - Klamath

Going for clams (Quinault)

On Quinault River

Quinault woman

Quinault berry picker

Quinault female

Quinault female

Quinault handiwork

Quinault houses

A mat shelter--Skokomish

A Skokomish Indian chief's daughter

Bahlkabuh (Skokomish)

Basket maker-Skokomish

Hleastunuh - Skokomish

Kalasetsah (Skokomish)

Lahkeudup (Skokomish)

Mat house - Skokomish

On Skokomish River

Skokomish baskets

Tsatsalatsa - Skokomish

Yalqablu (Skokomish)

At the spring (Wishham)

Dip-netting in pools - Wishham

Fish carrier - Wishham

Hlalakum - Wishham

Island of the dead (Wishham)

Kashhila - Wishham

Kyetani (Wishham)

NORTHWEST COAST AND CALIFORNIA

Mnashwai (Wishham)

On the Columbia (Wishham)

Petroglyphs (Wishham).

Pounding fish (Wishham)

Preparing salmon (Wishham)

Spearing salmon - Wishham

Spidis (Wishham)

The rock slide (Wishham)

Water baskets (Wishham)

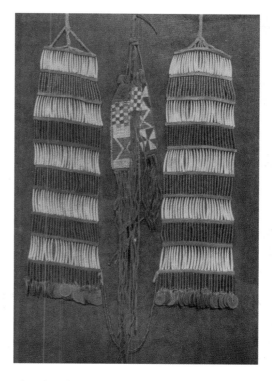

Whishham beadwork

Wishham basket worker

Wishham bowl

Wishham bride

Wishham child

Wishham girls

Wishham man

Wishham woman

Basin and Plateau

Great Basin

As the ancestral native Indian tribes moved south, many settled in a geophysical area known as the Great Basin. This region covers most of Utah and Nevada, as well as large parts of Colorado, Wyoming, Idaho, Oregon and California. Small parts of Arizona, New Mexico, and Montana also fall into this zone. As the Great Basin flattens out, it forms what is known as the Plateau region. This covers much of the Rocky Mountains in the north-western United States and runs into the southern parts of British Columbia. Since the two regions run into each other, they are often - like here, considered together.

The Great Basin is a harsh area to survive in - the lower altitudes are mostly comprised of desert vegetation such as sagebrush and tough grasses. The higher areas which bound much of the basin are largely mountain ranges covered with dry pine forests. This arid climate is due to the fact that on the eastern side of the region lie the Rocky Mountains, and on the western border there are the Sierra Nevadas. Together they form a barrier to most rain clouds, which results in a very low annual rainfall. Temperatures reach both extremes, getting very high in the summer, and very low in the winter.

In order to survive in the dry environment of the Great Basin with its sparse vegetation and few animals, the native Indians had to be adaptable, and most lived as typical hunter-gatherers. Although there was some game to be sought, fishing provided a large part of their protein intake. At the right times of year, the local tribes peoples were able to collect large quantities of pine nuts, as well as acorns, grass seeds, wild beans and many different kinds of berries. Where there was enough water to do so, some tribes also grew basic crops such as squash, corn and beans.

The lack of consistent resources meant that people were unable to assemble in any numbers except in times of plenty. As a result, most of the tribes lived semi-nomadic lifestyles, spending much of the year split into small family groups. These travelled widely looking for opportunities to gather food. When the times were right, however, large groups would get together for mass hunting sessions. Sometimes these would be to catch and feast on large grasshoppers, which would often collect in massive numbers. At other times they would organise drives to chase down larger animals such as rabbits or antelope.

Buffalo were the most sought after prey, however, they were too large and too fast to be caught in the open. A single animal would provide food for a family group for a long time, so when a herd was in the area, special drives would be set up. The most effective way of killing buffalo was simply to panic them into running over cliffs - their carcasses were then butchered and removed. All this changed when the horse was introduced. This gave the native Indians the chance to chase buffalo on the hoof - they could then get close enough to make a kill using the bow and arrow.

Basin and Plateau

The ability to travel long distances using horses meant that Great Basin tribes often ventured out onto the Plains in search of buffalo. If they were due to go hunting, it was customary to ask the spirits for good fortune - this was done by medicine men, who were also known as Shamans. These individuals were very powerful characters within the tribal system - not only did they perform special ceremonies, but they were also relied on to cure the sick and injured.

When a hunt was successful, not only were thanks made to the spirits, but good use was made of every last scrap of the animal. Meat was eaten or dried for later use. Fat was kept for waterproofing skins and for cooking. Wool was collected and used as insulation and for making simple textiles. Skins were made into clothes or in the construction of shelters called wickiups, which are winter dwellings that are more substantial than those used in the summer. They are small tepee-shaped structures made up of a framework of wooden poles covered with whatever came to hand. This could be anything from turf sods cut from the ground, to bark or brushwood, or indeed, animal hides. In the warmer months, the wickiups were dispensed with, and simple wind-breaks were made from brushwood. The simplicity of these structures meant they were very quick to construct. This allowed the tribes people the freedom to move around more easily, and they could focus on collecting food rather than building new labour-intensive homes every time they moved.

The clothes that were worn depended on the temperature. In the warmer areas men wore simple animal-skin breechcloths, and the women wore skirts. In the more northern regions, the clothes worn had to be much warmer to cope with the cold. Both men and women would wear leggings, but the women would wear long dresses over them whereas the men wore thick shirts.

While the introduction of horses was a great benefit to the native peoples of the Great Basin, the appearance of miners and settlers was not. The newcomers brought livestock that ate many of the plants the tribes people relied on for much of their food, but worse than this, when the forests were cut down to provide timber and firewood, they lost their source of pine nuts. This removed one of the mainstays of their existence, and times became very hard indeed. Things became even more difficult when gold and silver were discovered in the region - this brought hordes of new settlers to the area, which put more pressure on the natural resources.

One of the biggest problems that the influx of Europeans brought was disease - everything from smallpox and scarlet fever to influenza worked its way through the native tribes people, and countless lives were lost. These days things are much more stable - the native Indians have, in the main, sorted out their legal rights, and as such have full title to large areas of land. Many make their living as ranchers or by leasing out mineral rights to industry.

BASIN AND PLATEAU

PLATEAU

The Plateau region is extensive - it covers south-eastern British Columbia, the eastern part of Washington, the north-eastern and central parts of Oregon, as well as some of northern Idaho, western Montana, and a small part of northern California. Like the Great Basin - which forms the southern boundary, it is bounded on the west and east by two mountain ranges - these are the Cascades and the Rockies. Unlike the Great Basin which is largely desert, many parts of the Plateau region are wet places, since the mountains either side trap most of the rain clouds which form there. In these areas this results in a high annual precipitation - the water collects and runs into the many streams and rivers. The two biggest waterways are the Columbia and Fraser Rivers, however, there are many smaller ones. These include the Snake, Okanagon, Willamette and Kootenai rivers.

The wet climate is ideal for trees to grow in, and many grow to enormous heights - indeed, some of the tallest ones in the world are found here. They are mostly coniferous species, and include cedar spruce, hemlock, pine, and many others. Like most evergreen forests, the trees grow very close together, and very little light reaches the ground. As a result, under the cover of the canopy they are very dark places which support very little wildlife. Consequently, in the most wooded areas there are few animals for humans to hunt. Around the fringes, however, large mammals such as deer and elk flourish. The extensive forests of the upper Fraser River mark the northern limits of the Plateau. Not all the Plateau receives high rainfall, however, and in the drier areas sagebrush predominates. These regions are largely rolling hills - the vegetation is able to support a good number of antelope and jackrabbits, as well as many other small animal species.

Although the tribes people of the region hunted small game wherever it could be found, a large part of their diet consisted of fish - especially salmon, which were caught in the rich rivers which ran through the area. Some of them would be eaten on the spot, but most were dried and stored to be traded or eaten later. A large amount of gathering was also undertaken, with berries, nuts, roots and bulbs being collected when they were in season - these were also dried and stored whenever possible. Some tribes also made a special kind of bread by grinding up acorns.

The people of the Plateau region often lived in brush shelters or lean-to structures that were very similar to those of the Great Basin tribes. They also had more permanent homes which were half-buried lodges with conical roofs or, sometimes wooden long houses covered with tree bark.

When the horse arrived in the early eighteenth century, the Plateau tribes continued to hunt fish, but they were also able to chase down and kill buffalo. Not only did this give them the ability to feed their families more reliably, but it meant that they could travel further to trade goods. This resulted in significant cultural changes, as interactions with other tribes became more commonplace. The choice of materials for clothing became wider, and many went from wearing primitive fabrics made from rabbit skins or woven tree bark, to using much better things like deerskin.

Although the native Indians of the Plateau region generally got on well with white fur trappers and traders, relations went downhill when settlers and miners started taking their lands. They also suffered, like most of the other American tribes, when they were exposed to the virulent diseases brought over from Europe. Eventually wars broke out, as settlers and tribes peoples fought over native lands. The most famous were the Modoc War of 1872-1873 and the Nez Percé War of 1877. Most of the tribes of the Plateau region now live on reservations in Canada and the United States.

BANNOCK

LAP PA WIN SUE.
A DELAWARE CHIEF

The Bannock were a native Indian tribe who lived in large territories which covered parts of the northern Great Plains and the foothills of the Rocky Mountains. They were mostly based in the southern regions of what today is the state of Idaho, where their lifestyles and cultures were similar to those of most of the other Plains Indians. A reservation was created for the native Indians of Idaho in 1869 - this was called the Fort Hall Reservation. The Bannock tribe shared these government appointed lands with the Northern Shoshone - a tribe that they had close links with. There was a Bannock tribe uprising in 1878 in protest at the loss of hunting grounds - the American government put this down vigorously. A small number of the Bannock people have survived to this day, although they number less than 5,000.

CAYUSE

The Cayuse tribe originally inhabited parts of upper Oregon and south-eastern Washington along the Columbia River. The Cayuse had many enemies due to their habit of preying on smaller tribes in the region. They were a very proud tribe, and although they called themselves 'the Superior People', the neighbouring tribes referred to them as 'People of the Rocks'. Not all the other tribes were enemies - for instance, they had particularly good relations with the Nez Percé tribe. The Cayuse brought about their own demise as a free people - in 1847 they attacked a Christian mission and killed the missionaries after blaming them for an outbreak of disease. The local settlers were outraged and declared war on the tribe. After their defeat, the tribe were moved to the Umatilla Reservation in Oregon. These days only a few true Cayuse still survive, and most live on the reservation as part of the Umatilla Federation.

Cayuse Man

Cayuse Warrior

Cayuse Woman

BASIN AND PLATEAU

Cayuse Youth

Daughter of Tamahus

Holiday Trappings - Cayuse

Cayuse Woman in the Forest

Cayuse Child Learning to Ride

Cayuse Matron

Cayuse Woman With Her Proudly Decked Horse

BASIN AND PLATEAU

FLATHEAD OR SALISH

The Flathead tribe - also known as the Salish, formerly occupied northern areas of Washington and Idaho, western Montana, part of the coast of Oregon, the southeast part of Vancouver Island and most of southern mainland British Columbia. There were two distinct groups of Flathead peoples - one on the north-west Pacific coast, and the other from the interior plateau region. Their name derives from the fact that some of the other tribes of the Columbia River region practised head shaping, where infants had their heads bound with straps to alter the shape of the skull. As a result, they had pointed heads - this meant that the unmodified skulls of the Flatheads were perceived as culturally backward, and the name was therefore a term of derision. For most of their early history they were gatherers who collected berries and roots, but once they had made peace with the Blackfeet - whose territory stood between them and buffalo country, they adopted more of a Plains culture. In 1909 there were just over 10,000 plateau Flathead people living in the United States and Canada.

A drink (Flathead)

A flathead chief

Ahlahlemila (Flathead)

Big Knife - Flathead

By the river - Flathead

Door-of-lodge grizzly (Flathead)

Drying meat (Flathead)

Flathead buffalo-skin lodge

Flathead camp on Jocko River

Flathead camp

BASIN AND PLATEAU

Flathead chief

Flathead childhood

Flathead dance

Flathead female

Flathead horse trapping

Flathead maiden

Flathead mother

Flathead warrior

Flathead young woman

Jerking meat (Flathead)

Many Bears (Flathead)

Nine Pipes (Flathead)

Not Indian (Flathead)

Red Owl (Flathead)

Stormy day - Flathead

Flathead man

KLIKITAT

The Klikitat tribe were formed by ancestors who came from the Shahaptian-speaking peoples. They originally came from the Klickitat and Skamania Counties, in Washington State. The name was given to them by the Chinook Indians, and means 'beyond'. This refers to the fact that they lived on the other side of the Cascade Mountains from the Chinook. In the early 1800's it was estimated that there were about 700 members of the Klickitat tribe. They were very successful traders, an attribute that was helped by the fact that their tribal lands were between the Cascade Mountains and the coast. This allowed them to profitably transport all manner of goods back and forth. The remaining members of the tribe are now mostly living on the Yakima Reservation, in Washington State.

BASIN AND PLATEAU

A Klikitat Brave

Klikitat Basketry

Klikitat Squaw

Mitsa (Klikitat)

KUTENAI

LE COLLAT DU CHENE.
AN OSAGE CHIEF.

The Kutenai (also spelt Kootenai or Kootenay) formerly inhabited areas of northern Montana, northern Idaho, and south-east British Columbia. This region was known as the 'Kutenai', hence the tribe's name. They were split into two main groups - the Upper Kutenai occupied lands around the headwaters of the Columbia River, and the Lower Kutenai inhabited the region of the Lower Kutenai River. Before the introduction of the horse, the Kutenai lived as hunter-gatherers, but once they were able to chase buffalo from horseback they adopted a Plains Indian lifestyle. Their first consistent contact with Europeans was with traders from the North West Company, who established a trading post on the upper Saskatchewan River. A small group of Kutenai people live on the Flathead Reservation in north-west Montana.

A Kutenai man

A young Kutenai

Camp in the forest (Kutenai)

Country of the Kutenai

Dressing skins (Kutenai)

Embarking - Kutenai

Komitsa (Kutenai)

Kutenai camp

Kutenai canoe

Kutenai duck hunter

Kutenai woman

Kutenai girls at the lake-shore

Kutenai girls

Kutenai maiden

Kutenai man

Kutenai woman

Not Grizzly-bear (Kutenai)

On Flathead Lake (Kutenai)

On the shore of the lake - Kutenai

Rush gatherer - Kutenai

MONO

LITTLE CROW
A Sioux Chief
Philadelphia. Published by Key & Biddle.

There were two main branches of the Mono—the eastern or Owens Valley Paiute who lived in the southern Sierra Nevadas—and the Western Mono or Monache. These are a group of six small Shoshonean speaking tribes that are now part of the mixed Tula River Reservation group.

BASIN AND PLATEAU

A Lake Mono Basket Maker

A Mono Man

An Owens Valley Mono

A Mono House Near Independence

NEZ PERCÉ / SAHAPTIN

MA HAS KAH
CHIEF OF THE IOWAYS

The Nez Percé are also referred to as the Sahaptin, or Shahaptin peoples. In the early 1800's, they occupied lands in west Idaho, north-eastern Oregon, and south-eastern Washington. The name Nez Percé came from the French - it means 'pierced nose', and refers to the fact that some members of the tribe wore nose pendants. Their early culture was very much that of the hunter-gatherer - they fished for salmon, dug for roots, and hunted for small animals. Once they acquired the horse, however, they took on many of the Plains Indian practises such as hunting buffalo. They also became accomplished horse breeders and traders. They fared badly when the gold rush of the 1860s and 1870s brought thousands of miners and settlers onto their lands, and many territorial disputes resulted.

A Nez Perce

A typical Nez Perce

A young Nez Perce

A young warrior (Nez Perce)

Black Eagle - Nez Perce

Chief Joseph - Nez Perce

Grizzly-Bear Ferocious (Nez Perce)

Half Moon (Nez Perce)

Half-Shorn (Nez Perce)

Joseph (Nez Perce)

Joseph Dead Feast Lodge (Nez Perce)

Kulkultsalum (Nez Perce)

Last home of Joseph (Nez Perce)

Lawyer - Nez Perce

BASIN AND PLATEAU

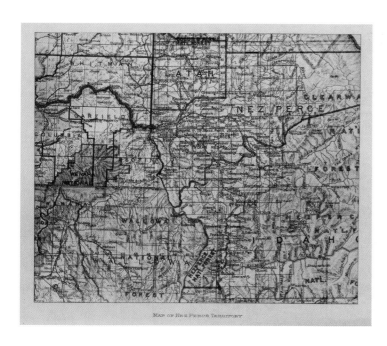

Map of the Nez Perce territory

Nez Perce babe

Nez Perce brave

Nez Perce canoe

Nez Perce girl

Nez Perce matron

Nez Perce profile

Nez Perce sweat-lodge

Nez Perce warrior

Nez Perce warrior

Night scout - Nez Perce

No Wings (Nez Perce)

On Klickitat River

Raven Blanket - Nez Perce

The old-time warrior (Nez Perce)

The scout (Nez Perce)

Three Eagles (Nez Perce)

Typical Nez Perce

PAIUTE

MAJOR RIDGE.
A CHEROKEE CHIEF.

The Paiute (also spelt 'Piute') tribe lived as two separate groups. The Northern Paiute inhabited the lands of central & eastern California, western Nevada, and eastern Oregon. The southern Paiute on the other hand lived in north-western Arizona, south-eastern California, southern Nevada, and southern Utah. Of the two groups the northern people were the more aggressive - they had many fights with settlers and miners during the mid 1800's. The southern Paiute had a completely different culture - they were hunter gatherers who got much of their food by digging for roots, as a result they were known as 'the diggers'. They would, however, also fish and hunt small animals when the opportunity presented itself. Today the remaining Paiute live on reservations in Arizona, California, Nevada, and Oregon.

Chemehuevi basketry

Chemehuevi granary

Primitive Chemehuevi dwelling

PLATEAU SHOSHONE

MAR-KO-ME-TE

A SHOSHONE BRAVE.

The Shoshone family is a group of associated native peoples that occupied the third largest tribal area in North America. At one time or another this region included south-western Montana, most of southern Idaho, all of Utah and Nevada, south-eastern Oregon, central and western Wyoming, central and western Colorado, much of New Mexico, and all of north-western Texas. Other Shoshonean lands included disjointed parts of California and northern Arizona. This massive area covers almost all the different kinds of climate and terrain that can be found between Mexico and Canada. Consequently, the various tribes that lived there had to adopt differing lifestyles to suit the kinds of environments they inhabited. Some were primarily hunters of large game animals, whereas others subsisted on roots, berries and small animals. The Shoshonean family itself was comprised of many tribes - these could be divided into three main groups. The first covers the Plateau Shoshoneans - the Chemehuevi, Kawaiisu, Paiute, Panamint, Ute, Comanche, Gosiute, Mono, Paviotso, part of the Bannock and the Shoshoneans of Eastern Oregon. The second group covers the Southern Californian Shoshoneans, and included the Serrano, Gabrieleño, Agua Caliente, Juaneño, Kawia, and Luiseño. The third group is made up of the Hopi peoples, who are considered to be distinct from the other two groups.

SPOKANE

The Spokane peoples occupied several small territories near the Spokane River in north-east Washington. Opinions differ as to how they should be classified - most authorities consider them to be distinct bands and not a single tribe. They lived in a manner typical of the plateau people, hunting and gathering as the opportunities arose. At the end of the nineteenth century they were given two reservations to live on - the Colville agency in Washington, and the Coeur d'Alene Reservation in Idaho. Their population has always been small, and between 1800 and 1910 it varied from around 400 to about 600. This has since risen to around 2,000, with members living on both the reserves in Washington and also in Idaho and Montana.

A hill camp (Spokan)

Author's camp among the Spokan

In the mountains (Spokan)

On the move (Spokan)

Pukimanstula (Spokan)

Returning to camp (Spokan)

spokan annie warner

Spokan camp

spokan coeur d alene

spokan joe moses

spokan man and two women

spokan man and woman

Spokan man

Spokan matron

spokan mother and child

Spokan woman

Spokan woman

UMATILLA

META- KOOSEGA
Pure Tobacco
A Chippeway Warrior

The Umatilla are a tribe from the Shahaptian linguistic family, although their own language is distinct from the others. They originally inhabited parts of the Columbia River Plateau in north-eastern Oregon and south-eastern Washington, along the banks of the Columbia River. In 1855, however, they agreed to a treaty whereby they were given the Umatilla Reservation in eastern Oregon to live on. They banded together with the Cayuse and Walla Walla Tribes to form the Confederated Tribes of the Umatilla Indian Reservation. It is difficult to know exactly how many members of the tribe still survive due to the continued presence of the other tribes who still also live on the same reservation. Estimates put the number of true blood Umatilla at 250 or less, although the confederation as a whole currently numbers around 2,500 people.

A mat lodge (Umatilla)

A mountain home (Umatilla)

A young Umatilla

fish hawk a famous umatilla indian

BASIN AND PLATEAU

Umatilla child

Umatilla child

Umatilla girl

White Bull (Umatilla)

UTE

DIE MA WA.
A CREEK WARRIOR.

The Ute tribe originally inhabited Colorado and eastern Utah, however, once they obtained horses they moved further afield and started hunting through Mexico and Arizona. They were fierce warriors who often raided and sometimes destroyed the villages of the Pueblo peoples. They became slave traders, capturing members of other tribes and selling them in slave markets in New Mexico. They were relocated onto a reservation in Colorado in 1868, and then moved again in 1880 as it was found that the land they were on was rich in minerals. Most of the remaining Ute live on reservations in Colorado and Utah, where they earn money by leasing land for oil and gas extraction as well as by more traditional methods such as farming.

ute burial ground

ute chief ignacio

ute horse drawn cart

ute indian abodes

ute men at tepee

ute standing wolf

Ute Chief Tabby

Ute Indians

Ute Indians with Horses

Ute Policeman

ute ward joe smith hallignacio mariana

ute womantannah

WALLA WALLA ('LITTLE RIVER')

ME-TE-A,
A POTTAWATOMIE CHIEF.

The Walla Walla are another tribe from the Shahaptian linguistic family. They originally lived in Washington and Oregon on the lower Walla Walla river and along the eastern bank of the Columbia River. Their language is a distinct dialect that is most closely related to that of the Nez Percé. They agreed to be moved to the Umatilla Indian Reservation in 1855, where it is thought the current population is around 460. This reserve covers around 160,000 acres. Over the years, however, they have inter-married with members of the Nez Percé, Cayuse and Umatilla tribes, so it is possible that the true blood line may not exist anymore.

YAKIMA

MICANOPY
A SEMINOLE CHIEF.

The Yakima used to inhabit lands along the Columbia and Yakima rivers, in central Washington.

They lived as typical hunter gatherers, and subsisted on various foodstuffs including salmon and many kinds of roots, berries, fruits and nuts. When the United States government tried to move them off their lands and onto a reservation in 1855, the Yakima initially agreed to do so. When they discovered that the authorities had tricked them, they started a war. This continued until 1859, when they finally agreed to move to a 1,130,000 acre reservation in south-western Washington State. They used to refer to themselves as ' Toppenish', however, in the 1990s they re-named the tribe the 'Yakama', as it fits the pronunciation more accurately. These days they generate most of their income through forestry.

A holiday lodge (Yakima)

A young Yakima

Camp of the Yakima

Camp of the root diggers (Yakima)

Deserted lodge (Yakima)

Drying piage (Yakima)

Inashah - Yakima

Lishhaiahit (Kittitas)

Luqaiot - Kittitas

Mat lodge (Yakima)

Mountain camp - Yakima

Sons of a Yakima chief

The root digger (Yakima)

Wife of Mnainak - Yakima

Chief of the land (Kalispel)

Crossing the Pend d'Oreille (Kalispel)

Dusty dress - Kalispel

Home of the Kalispel

Kalispel camp

Kalispel canoes

Kalispel maiden

Kalispel scene

Kalispel village

Kalispel youth

Masselow, Kalispel chief

On the Pend d'Oreille (Kalispel)

Shirt (Kalispel)

The chief's wife (Kalispel)

The peace-officer (Kalispel)

Touch Her Dress (Kalispel)

Nespilim Girl

Nespilim Man

Nespilim Girl

On Nespilim Creek

PLAIN AND PRAIRIE

The Great Plains culture area is a vast grassland which stretches from the west of the Mississippi Valley across to the foothills on the eastern side of the Rocky Mountains. It is bounded in the north by the Canadian Provinces of Manitoba, Saskatchewan and Alberta. The southern boundary is formed by the state of Texas. Most of the area is open grassland, however, where there are rivers and streams there are many small stands of willows and cottonwood trees. There are also several mountain ranges in the region. These include the Ozarks in Missouri, the Badlands of North Dakota, and the Black Hills of South Dakota and Wyoming.

Before the arrival of Europeans - an era known as 'pre-Columbian', the native tribes fell into two main categories - those that were nomadic and those that were sedentary. The nomads moved around on foot following the buffalo herds. They often used bush fires to force the herds into enclosures where they could be easily killed. This was a harsh existence, since it was very hard to keep pace with the herds, and many drives failed. As a result, the natives went through cycles of hunger and plenty. When a drive was successful, they were able to trade the meat and skins with local farming tribes for grain and other crops.

The tribes that chose to create permanent settlements did so where the ground was suitable for farming corn, various kinds of beans and squash - this was mostly in the valleys of the great rivers. They built substantial homes to house their extended families - these were dome-shaped lodges with thick walls constructed from compacted mud. For protection from the strong winds and enemy attack, most of these villages were surrounded by massive earthen walls. While many of the native tribes lived in this way, some, such as the Mandan tribe were semi-nomadic, and also used tepees when they left their villages to go hunting. These were tent-like conical structures made of poles and covered with buffalo skin.

On the eastern side of the region where the rainfall is heaviest - between 20 and 40 inches annually, the prairie grasses grow very tall. Towards the western areas, however, the rainfall is much lower - about 10 - 20 inches annually, and this results in the grasses being much shorter. The prairies are ideal grazing grounds for herbivorous animals - none more so than the buffalo. As the last ice-age receded, these large animals flourished in the enormity of the grasslands. Since their main natural predators died out with the climatic changes at the end of the ice-age, they increased in numbers such that when the first Europeans arrived, a single herd could stretch from horizon to horizon.

As with the native tribes in the other culture areas that had access to buffalo, these animals represented not only a supply of meat, but also a source of many other vital commodities. Until the horse was introduced by Spanish explorers, the Plains Indians had to hunt on foot - this meant they could only manage to make the occasional kill. Once they were mounted on horseback, however, they were able to chase and kill as many buffalo as they wanted. Any meat that wasn't destined to be eaten in the short term was cut and pounded into flat strips and then dried. In this state it could be stored to be used later, or traded for other commodities.

The transition from foot to horseback happened around the early 1700's. It marked a profound change in the lifestyles of almost all the native tribes in the region. Many of the previously sedentary peoples found that because horses gave them the ability to keep up with the buffalo herds, it was more productive to hunt than to farm. As a result a lot of them gave up farming and took to a nomadic hunter-gatherer lifestyle instead. Exceptions to this were the Arikara, the Hidatsa, and the Mandan tribes.

It is important to realise that the native Indian perspective on the connection between the spirit world and the their own meant that every animal was seen as sacred. This had important implications for the buffalo herds, as the native hunters would only kill what they needed, and no more. Once the Europeans came on the scene, however, they viewed the seemingly endless herds as an infinite resource, and they killed everything in sight. Before long the numbers of buffalo had reduced to the point where they were facing extinction. Fortunately, action was taken in time and their populations are now increasing, although most of their original habitats have since become farmland.

The history of the tribes of the Great Plains and Prairie culture region is long and complicated. It can be divided up into three main periods. The first is the era of hardship before the advent of the horse - this is from antiquity to the late 1600's. The second is the time of plenty after horses were obtained in the early 1700's, but before European settlers made their mark. The third is the post-conquest period from when settlers took control of the region in the mid 1800's, up to the present day.

PLAIN AND PRAIRIE

The tribes that roamed the plains on horseback following the herds of buffalo were generally made up of groups of related families. During the winter these groups would split up and the families would each go off on their own to look for food, but in the summer they would assemble again to hunt for buffalo. These were also times when religious celebrations would be held - the native Indian peoples were very spiritual, and generally believed in personal spirit guides. These guides would visit them during vision quests, which were ritual events held to commune with the spiritual world. Some tribes used 'medicine bundles' - these were sacred pouches carried by certain members of the tribe, and which contained various objects that it was believed possessed special powers. These could be plants, stones, or artefacts that for one reason or another were judged to have the necessary spiritual significance.

The Sun Dance was a particularly important religious ceremony to the tribes of the Great Plains. It was the time when thanks were made for the good things that happened in the last year, and blessings were asked for the forthcoming year. This and other rituals are still performed to this day by many of the Plains Indian tribes.

Some people refer to the Plains region as one entity, whereas others maintain that the cultures of the semi-nomadic farmers on the prairies and those of the hunters on the plains are so different that the culture area needs to be treated as two separate regions - the Plains and Prairie. In this case the dividing line is the course of the Lower Mississippi and central Missouri Rivers.

Many of the earliest native tribes to settle in the region established farming communities - this was because hunting on foot on the plains was usually very unproductive. Growing food was therefore considered to be a much more reliable way of feeding their families. Such tribes included the Mandan and Hidatsa (who spoke Siouan languages), and the Wichita, Pawnee and Arikara (who spoke variants of the Caddoan language family).

With the arrival of the horse, other tribes moved in from the east lured by the enormous herds of buffalo. These included the Arapaho, Cheyenne, Crow, Gros Ventre, Osage, Otoe, Quapaw, and Sioux peoples. Many of these tribes made the move onto the plains because they were feeling the pressure of the European settlers who were moving onto their traditional homelands. On top of this there were many severe droughts in the eastern lands - the horse opened up the potential of hunting buffalo instead of fighting the settlers. It was not only from the east that new native tribes came in search of buffalo - the Sioux moved in from the Great Lakes area, and the Comanche and Kiowa moved onto the plains from the west and north-west. The Navajo and the Apache moved up from the south-west.

The diversity and complexity of the languages in the region meant that communication was very difficult. This made trading or simply remaining on good terms with your neighbours a confusing affair. As a result, a simple universal sign language was developed, and this became popular throughout the culture area.

When the European settlers reached the plains the only true nomads were the Blackfeet tribes in the northern parts of the region and the Comanche in the southern areas. All the others were either farmers in permanent villages, or semi-nomadic tribes who returned to more permanent settlements between excursions.

The plains Indians were among the last to carry on fighting the settlers - in 1890, this culminated in the battle of Wounded Knee, South Dakota, where the Federal soldiers of the U.S. Army massacred as many as 300 Sioux men, women and children. After this the plains Indians became the focus of much media attention, and thus the public came to associate all native Americans with those from the plains.

These days things have changed - for instance, many Sioux members are now heavily involved in the American Indian Movement, which is an organisation that fights for the native American's legal and civil rights. Others, including many members of the Cheyenne and Comanche tribes are now playing leading roles in the Native American Church.

There are three main language families in the Plains and Prairie culture area - these are the Algonquian-Wakashan, the Aztec-Tanoan, and the Hokan-Siouan.

ARAPAHO

MLSTIPPEE.

The Arapaho (also spelt 'Arapahoe', 'Arrapaho', or 'Arrapahoe') are thought to have migrated onto the Plains area from the Red River Valley in North Minnesota. Evidence also suggests that they are closely related to the Blackfoot and Cheyenne peoples, however, little is actually known of their early history. Although they called themselves the 'Inuna-ina' which translates as 'our people', other tribes labelled them after one of their culinary habits as the 'dog eaters'. At some stage after their arrival on the plains, they split into three groups – these were the Gros Ventre, the Northern Arapaho and the Southern Arapaho.

The Northern Arapaho group – who are considered to be the parent group from which the others split, remained in the area around the North Platte River in Wyoming. In 1876, they were moved to the Wind River Reservation in Wyoming, where they now live alongside their former enemies, the Shoshone.

The Southern Arapaho, who settled around the Arkansas River in Colorado are now living with the Cheyenne in Oklahoma. The Gros Ventre (which translates from the French as 'Big Belly') were split into two further groups – these were the Atsina and the Hidatsa (also spelt 'Hinatsa'). The Atsina were originally allied with the Blackfoot tribe; these days there are around 2,800 surviving members, most of whom live with the Assiniboin on the Fort Belknap Reservation in Montana. The Hidatsa (who were also known as the 'Minitari') lived in settlements composed of round houses made from mud, around which was a large earthen wall. They obtained their primary foodstuffs by farming corn and hunting for buffalo. The tribe was badly hit by a smallpox epidemic in 1837, after which they moved up the Missouri River and settled near the Fort Berthold trading post in North Dakota where many of their descendants still live.

A Good Man (Arapaho)

A Smoke (Arapaho)

Arapaho Camp

Arapaho Water Girl

Aapaho Youth

Eagle Chief (Arapaho)

Mother and Child (Arapaho)

The Ancient Arapaho

Plain and Prairie

Arikara or Ree

The Arikara (also spelt 'Arikari') originally occupied homelands along the course of the upper Missouri River – it is believed they settled there at least as early as the 1300s. They were a semi-sedentary group who lived in earth-covered lodges during the spring and summer. During these months they tended their crops of corn, beans and squash. Surplus foods were traded with other tribes for buffalo meat and hides. When the colder weather arrived, they would de-camp and track the buffalo herds. They were moved to the Fort Berthold Reservation in North Dakota in the late 1800s, where many of them still reside alongside the Mandan and the Hidatsa tribes.

Arikara chief

Arikara corn ceremony bearing out the osiers

Arikara girl

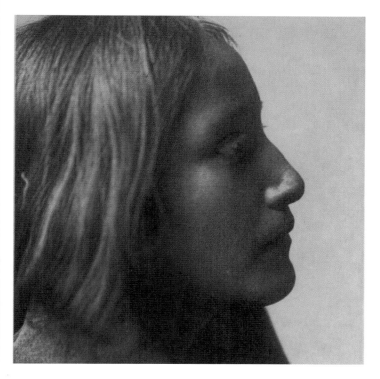

Arikara maiden

Arikara medicine ceremony Bear, buffalo, and night men

Arikara medicine ceremony The bears

Arikara medicine ceremony The buffalo dancing

Arikara medicine ceremony - The Bears

Arikara medicine ceremony - The Ducks

Arikara medicine ceremony Night men dancing

Arikara medicine ceremony The buffalo

Arikara medicine ceremony. Dance of the black-tail deer

Arikara medicine ceremony. Dance of the fraternity

Arikara medicine fraternity - The prayer

Arikara medicine fraternity

Arikara medicine-lodge

Arikara summer home

Arikara woman

Bear's Belly - Arikara

Bear's Teeth - Arikara

Blessing the children (Arikara)

Bringing in the cedar (Arikara)

Bull Neck - Arikara

Camp gossips (Arikara)

Contents of Arikara tribal medicine bundle

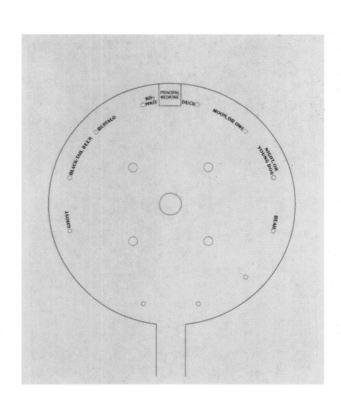

Dancing into the medicine-lodge (Arikara)

Four Horns - Arikara

Ground plan of Arikara medicine-lodge

In the medicine-lodge (Arikara)

Keeper of a medicine bundle (Arikara)

Little Sioux - Arikara

Medicine bundles (Arikara)

Rattles of Arikara bear medicine-men

Rush gatherer - Arikara

Sitting Bear - Arikara

The altar (Arikara)

The bear emerges (Arikara)

The brush-gatherers (Arikara)

PLAIN AND PRAIRIE

ASSINIBOINE AND STONEY

MOA-NA-HON-GA.
Great Walker.
AN IOWAY CHIEF.

The Assiniboin formerly inhabited the valley regions of the Saskatchewan and Assiniboin Rivers, in Canada. Later they moved to central North America, in and around the area of northern Minnesota, a land of coniferous forests and numerous lakes. Their name translates from a Chippewa expression as 'one who cooks with heated stones'. They have also been referred to by several other names – the Hidatsa referred to them as 'long arrows', the French as 'rebels', the English as 'Stone Indians', and the Kutenai as 'cut-throats'. The Assiniboin did not build permanent houses as they had a nomadic lifestyle, and lived in tipis, which were lightweight tents made from a skin-covered framework of poles. These were made so that they were easy to set up and take down in a hurry – a vital attribute as for much of the year the tribe had to move constantly to follow the buffalo herds. Some of the tented settlements were quite large, and could be composed of up to 200 tipis - the bigger ones often housed more than one family. During the winter the tented villages moved less frequently, as the animals they hunted did not move across large distances in the same way as buffalo did. In these cold months their quarry would mostly be composed of antelope, deer, elk and bighorn sheep. While the men were out hunting, the women would collect berries, roots, nuts and fruit. Although the Assiniboin were one of the largest tribes in the region, when smallpox brought by white settlers hit them, many thousands died. This reduced them to the point where they were unable to protest when they were forced onto a reservation in western Montana. If this state of affairs was not bad enough, the United States government failed to deliver promised food supplies, and many hundreds more starved to death. The remnant of the tribe now live on reservation lands in Canada and Montana.

An Assiniboin Lodge

Assiniboin Camp

Black Eagle - Assiniboin

Long Fox - Assiniboin

BLACKFOOT OR BLACKFEET

The Blackfoot, who are also known as the 'Blackfeet', were a group of Plains Indians that were composed of three main tribes. These were the Siksika, (also spelt 'Siksikawa', who are considered to be the 'true' Blackfoot), the Piegan, and the Kainah. The name 'Piegan' translates as 'people having badly dressed robes', and the word Kainah means 'Blood'. In the early 1800s they inhabited lands that ranged across a wide area around the Upper Missouri and North Saskatchewan rivers, and west as far as the Rockies. The name 'Blackfoot' was applied to them because they used to dye their moccasins black. The tribe were nomadic, and very hostile to almost all of the other local native peoples, they did, however, form a close alliance with the unrelated Atsina tribe. They were also usually aggressive towards white settlers, but in spite of this, they grew rich by doing business with European traders. The lucrative deals they did revolved around exchanging beaver pelts for firearms and other modern commodities. Things soon started to go badly wrong for them in the mid 1800s though. This was because the large numbers of white hunters who came into the area armed with powerful guns reduced the populations of buffalo and beaver so far that the Blackfoot people were left with no furs to trade and no meat to eat. This put them in a very difficult situation, and many of their people suffered as a result – their tribe fell from 3,700 in 1858, but 3 years later this had fallen to around 2,500. These days their descendants live on reservations in Montana and Alberta.

A Blackfoot ceremonial bag

A Blackfoot soldier

A Blackfoot travois

A Blackfoot

A beaver-bundle (Blackfoot)

A medicine-bag (Blackfoot)

A typical Blackfoot

Blackfoot cookery

Blackfoot country

Blackfoot finery

Blackfoot war-bonnet

Bow River and the sandhills (Blackfoot)

Fat horse, with insignia of a Blackfoot soldier

Fleshing a hide - Blackfoot

CHEYENNE

The Cheyenne (also spelt 'Cheyanne') formerly inhabited lands in the Minnesota region, however, problems with the Sioux and Ojibwa tribes in the 1600s forced them to move south-west to avoid further conflict. After this time they acquired the horse, and they became nomadic buffalo hunters who ranged far and wide across the plains in search of their quarry. In the early 1800s they split into two groups – these were the Northern and the Southern Cheyenne. The Northern group stayed in the territories they had occupied along the upper River Platte since moving away from Minnesota 200 years earlier. The Southern group, however, settled along the Arkansas river, where they allied with the Arapaho and engaged in constant warfare against the Kiowa, Comanche, and Apache. A peace treaty was finally brokered around 1840, whereupon the five tribes became allies. Although they were hostile towards many of the other native tribes, they generally got on well with the white settlers. This changed when the gold rush brought large numbers of rough gold seekers onto their territories. In the early 1860s the Cheyenne were forced to accept relocation onto a reservation in Oklahoma, however, the authorities failed to deliver their promises, and the tribe starved. In order to feed their people, they raided many local farms, but in 1864, in response to this the U.S. Army massacred a large number of defenceless Cheyenne people, including men, women and children at Sand Creek, Colorado. The conflict waged on for years, and culminated in 1876 at the famous Battle of the Little Bighorn, where the Northern Cheyenne aided by the Sioux massacred General Custer and the 7th Cavalry. After this they were defeated and moved onto the same reservation in Oklahoma as the Southern Cheyenne. This was a very difficult time for them, and their numbers fell drastically as a result of disease and malnutrition. Today most of the tribe are settled on a reservation in Montana.

Animal dance (Cheyenne)

At the ford - Cheyenne

Beginning of the altar (Cheyenne)

Boughs for the altar (Cheyenne)

Building the sun lodge (Cheyenne)

Camp in the cottonwoods - Cheyenne

Cheyenne female profile

Cheyenne female

Cheyenne girl

Cheyenne man

Cheyenne matron

Cheyenne profile

Cheyenne

Cheyenne warriors

Cheyenne woman

Cheyenne young woman

Crazy dancers (Cheyenne)

Dancing (Cheyenne)

Departure from preparation lodge (Cheyenne)

Devotees en route (Cheyenne)

Gray Dawn (Cheyenne)

PLAIN AND PRAIRIE

Lame deer monuments (Cheyenne)

Little Wolf - Cheyenne

Offering pipe to the earth (Cheyenne)

Offering pipe to the skull (Cheyenne)

Painting the poles (Cheyenne)

Piegan camp

Porcupine - Cheyenne

Priests passing before the pipe (Cheyenne)

Red Plume (Piegan)

Return of scouts (Cheyenne)

Return with boughs (Cheyenne)

Stone grave (Cheyenne)

Sun dance in progress (Cheyenne)

Sun dance pledgers (Cheyenne)

Sweat-lodge frame (Cheyenne)

The altar (Cheyenne)

Two Moons - Cheyenne

COMMANCHE

The Comanche were a tribe that originally had a culture typical of the Basin Indians, however, when they acquired the horse, they split from the Shoshone tribe and moved southward to New Mexico, where they soon evolved a Plains culture. By the late 1700s their territories covered south-east Colorado, south-west Kansas, western Oklahoma, and northern Texas. They refer to themselves as Numunuh, which means 'The People', however, the name 'Comanche' is derived from 'Komantcia', which was the name the Spanish used for them. This word means 'anyone who wants to fight me all the time'. It is not surprising, therefore, that they were a very warlike people. They often went on long distance raids that even reached as far south as Mexico, and it is said that for their size they killed more white people than any other native Indian group. They were superb horsemen, and this combined with their aggression prevented white settlers from travelling across their lands for over a hundred years. Their population suffered badly from introduced European diseases as well as from losses experienced as a result of warfare, and their numbers fell dramatically.

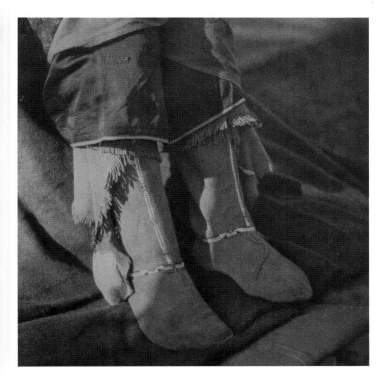

Comanche footwear

Comanche mothers

Esipermi - Comanche

Kicha (Comanche)

Pakewa (Comanche)

Wilbur Peebo (Comanche)

comanche Choppy wife of Paafybitty

comanche ester clark

comanche men Too-ah-nipper standing

comanche men backdrop

comanche nau nooh

comanche peets nah

comanche ti suy o son of chief nowway

comanche wife of oscar yellow wolf

comanche women and old man pueblo

comanche women

CROW

The Crow Indians originally inhabited lands around the upper Missouri River until they moved westwards in the early 1700s before finally settling in the Wyoming area. Their culture was that of Plains Indians, with their lives being focused on hunting buffalo. They did, however, plant crops of tobacco which was an important part of their complex religious and social activities. The Crow were long-term enemies of the Sioux tribe, and were also aggressive towards the first groups of European settlers who travelled along the Oregon Trail. Although they continued to fight the Sioux, after a while they made peace with the white pioneers, and became close allies of the U.S. Army in the Sioux Wars. Many Crow warriors became scouts, and some served with the Seventh Cavalry under General Custer. These days most of the 9,000 or so Crow peoples live on a large reservation to the north of the Montana-Wyoming border, where many earn a good living through ranching, and tourism, as well as by leasing out rights for extracting mineral resources.

A baby Apsaroke

A burial platform (Apsaroke)

A winter day (Apsaroke)

PLAIN AND PRAIRIE

An Apsaroke lodge

Approaching winter (Apsaroke)

Apsaroke camp

Apsaroke horse trappings

Apsaroke maiden

Apsaroke medicine tipi

Apsaroke mother

Apsaroke war group

Apsaroke war-chief

Apsaroke woman

Apsaroke youths

Autumn - Apsaroke

Big Ox (Apsaroke)

Bird On The Ground (Apsaroke)

Bull Chief - Apsaroke

Bread - Apsaroke

Bull Goes Hunting (Apsaroke)

Bull Tongue (Apsaroke)

Chief and his staff - Apsaroke

Coups Well-Known - Apsaroke

Does Everything (Apsaroke)

Fish Shows - Apsaroke

Flathead woman (Apsaroke)

Fog in the morning (Apsaroke)

For a winter campaign - Apsaroke

Goes Ahead (Apsaroke)

Going to camp - Apsaroke

Hairy Moccasins (Apsaroke)

Hide scraping (Apsaroke)

Hide stretching (Apsaroke)

Hoop On The Forehead - Apsaroke

Hunts The Enemy (Apsaroke)

Hunts To Die (Apsaroke)

In Black Canyon - Apsaroke

In the canyon (Apsaroke)

Medicine tripod (Apsaroke)

Medicine Crow - Apsaroke

Medicine lodge (Apsaroke)

Mother and child (Apsaroke)

Mountain fastness - Apsaroke

Moving (Apsaroke)

PLAIN AND PRAIRIE

Old Dog (Apsaroke)

On Top (Apsaroke)

On the Little Bighorn - Apsaroke

Packhorse (Apsaroke)

Passing the cliff - Apsaroke

Playmates (Apsaroke)

Plenty Coups - Apsaroke

Ready for the charge - Apsaroke

Red Wing - Apsaroke

Scaffold burial (Apsaroke)

Scout in winter - Apsaroke

Shot In The Hand - Apsaroke

Sisters (Apsaroke)

Sitting Elk - Apsaroke

Skins Wolf (Apsaroke)

Spirit of the past - Apsaroke

Spotted Jack-Rabbit (Apsaroke)

Successful raid for the horses - Apsaroke

Swallow Bird - Apsaroke

Sweat-lodge (Apsaroke)

The eagle medicine-man (Apsaroke)

The lookout (Apsaroke)

The oath (Apsaroke)

The parade (Apsaroke)

The scout (Apsaroke)

The sun dance votary (Apsaroke)

The sun dancer (Apsaroke)

The winter camp (Apsaroke)

Tobacco ceremonial lodge (Apsaroke)

Tobacco ceremony (Apsaroke)

Two Leggings - Apsaroke

Two Leggings Lodge (Apsaroke)

Two Whistles - Apsaroke

Upshaw - Apsaroke

Watching for the signal - Apsaroke

Wet - Apsaroke

GROS VENTRE OR ATSINA

Also known as the Atsina, the Gros Ventre were once considered part of the Arapaho. Close allies of the Blackfeet, their history is closely interwoven with their powerful neighbours. Today they share the Fort Belknap Reservation with the Assiniboine.

Assiniboin boy - Atsina

Atsina Indian on horse pulling travois

Atsina Indian, Red Whip

Atsina burial-ground

Atsina burial

Atsina camp scene

Atsina camp

Atsina chiefs

Atsina crazy dance A dancer kisses the grandfather

Atsina crazy dance The flight of arrows

Atsina crazy dancers

Atsina fly dance Robes outstretched

Atsina fly dance

Atsina maiden

Atsina scalp dance

Atsina war-party

Atsina warriors

Awaiting the scouts' return

Crow Ghost (Arikara)

Curly Head (Atsina)

Cuts Tether (Atsina)

Eagle Child - Atsina

Lone Flag - Atsina

Head-dress - Atsina

Making a travois (Atsina)

Horse Capture - Atsina

Incense (Atsina)

Land of the Atsina

Moving camp (Atsina)

No Bear - Atsina

On the war-path - Atsina

Otter Robe - Atsina

Parfleches (Atsina)

Red Star (Arikara)

Red Whip - Atsina

Running Fisher (Atsina)

Scout - Atsina

Scout's report - Atsina

Singing in the crazy dance (Atsina)

Singing to the cedar (Arikara)

The halt (Atsina)

The pipe-bearer (Atsina)

HIDATSA

MON-CHONSIA.
A KANSAS CHIEF.

The Hidatsa or Minitaree is a Siouan tribe that was badly affected by smallpox in 1837. Sometimes called the Gros Ventre of the Missouri—and confused with that tribe—they were an earth-lodge dwelling people and thus became the intermediaries between the Plains nomads and the fur trade. They were visited by Lewis and Clarke's expedition and moved to Fort Berthold after the epidemic. They are still there, closely linked with the Mandan.

Good Bear (Hidatsa)

Hidatsa bull-boat

Hidatsa man

Hidatsa mother

Hidatsa woman

Holds The Eagle (Hidatsa)

Incense over a medicine bundle (Hidatsa)

Lean Wolf (Hidatsa)

Long-time Dog (Hidatsa)

Rabbit-Head (Hidatsa)

Site of abandoned Hidatsa Village

Sitting Owl (Hidatsa)

IOWA

It is thought that the Iowa (also spelt 'Ioway') were originally part of the Winnebago peoples when they lived in the area north of the Great Lakes. It is known that by 1700 they were living in Minnesota when their population was around the 1,100 mark, but after a particularly bad epidemic of smallpox, they moved again. By the early 1800s their numbers had fallen to about 800 individuals, and they were inhabiting lands in the region of the Platte River. The United States authorities took advantage of their weakened state, and in 1824, forced the Iowa tribe to hand over all their territories in Missouri. Instead they were given a reservation in north-east Kansas, although some of the tribe later chose to move to Oklahoma.

KIOWA

NAH-ET-LUC-HOPIE.

The Kiowa were a nomadic people of the Plains who lived in West Montana in the early 1600s, however, by the start of the 1700s they had settled in a region to the south-east of the Yellowstone River. The Crow tribe gave them permission to live in the Black Hills, however, the Cheyenne and Sioux tribes drove them out of the area and they had to move south to avoid further conflict. They took up residence in territories that belonged to the Comanche - with whom they soon ended up in a state of warfare. After much violence between the two peoples, a permanent peace settlement was eventually agreed in 1790. In the early 1800s the Kiowa moved to lands in the region of the Arkansas River. In the course of the next three decades they formed an alliance with the Comanche, and took part in a lot of long-distance raiding parties. They were very hostile to white settlers, and many conflicts occurred during this time. The U.S. government finally managed to put a stop to most of the aggression in the late 1830s, when a treaty to allow the passage of white pioneers across their lands was agreed. After this the Kiowa - in alliance with several other tribes, started to fight the Indians who had been forced to move to Oklahoma by the government. This continued for a long time, but in the end the U.S. Army managed to defeat the alliance and the Treaty of Medicine was imposed on them in 1867. By the end of the 1870s most of the Kiowa had moved to a reservation in Oklahoma where many of their descendants still live.

kiowa lone wolfs son

kiowa running horse

kiowa sgt. i see o indian scout

kiowa ah ta pe

kiowa lone wolf and wife

kiowa portrait

MANDAN

In the mid 1700s, the Mandan lived in the region of the mouth of the Heart River in south-central North Dakota, where they had a collection of nine settlements. It is believed, however, that they originally came from further east than this. They were weakened by epidemics of smallpox, and this left them open to attacks by the Assiniboin and the Sioux tribes. To escape further hostilities they moved up the Missouri River and settled near the Arikara tribe around the Knife River. The Mandan numbered around 1,250 individuals in the early 1800s, but by the late 1830s disease had reduced their population to only 150. They were allies of the Hidatsa, and in 1845 both tribes moved to the Fort Berthold trading post in North Dakota. In 1870 a large reservation was created for the Mandan, Arikara and Hidatsa tribes to share.

Buffalo dance costume (Mandan)

Buffalo dancer (Mandan)

Buffalo-berry gatherers (Mandan)

Contents of bundle of Numak-Mahana (Mandan)

Crow's Heart (Mandan)

Cutting rushes (Mandan)

Mandan bull-boat

Mandan earthen lodge

Mandan girl

Numak-Mahana

Offering the buffalo-skull (Mandan)

Packs Wolf As Numak-Mahana (Mandan)

Ready for Okipe buffalo dance (Mandan)

Record of custodians of a turtle-drum (Mandan)

Scattered Corn Woman (Mandan)

Spotted Bull - Mandan

Omaha

NEA - MATH - LA,
A OMAHA CHIEF.

The Omaha were a typical Plains Indian tribe who were closely associated with the Ponca peoples. Both groups originally lived in the Ohio Valley, but moved together to the area around the junction of the Missouri and Mississippi rivers. Not long after this they continued on to Iowa, but after suffering a severe epidemic of smallpox in 1802, they settled in north-east Nebraska. In the winter the tribe lived in lodges which had thick mud walls to keep them warm. In the summer, however, they used lightweight tipis. The Omaha had a long series of wars with the Sioux Nation, but in 1854 they were forced to give up their lands and move to Dakota County, Nebraska. Although the tribe were given the rights to purchase their own lands as individuals in 1882, many chose instead to remain on the reservation.

OSAGE

NE O MON NI,
AN IOWAY CHIEF

The ancestors of the Osage tribe inhabited lands in the Ohio Valley, but by the end of the 1600s they had moved to the region around the Osage River in Missouri. There were three different divisions within the Osage group; in 1802 they numbered together around 5,500 people. The Osage were an aggressive peoples who often conducted wars against other local tribes. They were typical Plains Indians, leading a semi-nomadic lifestyle centred on hunting game animals and gathering wild produce; they also cultivated a few crops. In 1810, the United States government forced the Osage to hand over their lands in Missouri, Arkansas, and Oklahoma. They were relocated on reservations in north-central Oklahoma and south-eastern Kansas; it was later found that on these lands there were extensive oilfields. This has made the 10,000 or so surviving tribal members the richest of the native peoples in North America.

OTO

NE SOU A QUOIT
A FOX CHIEF

The Oto (also spelt 'Otoe') – along with the Iowa and Missouri tribes were once part of the Winnebago nation, at which time they lived north of the Great Lakes. When the Oto left this area, the Missouri went with them, but they soon argued, and the two tribes went their separate ways thereafter. The Oto established a typical Plains Indian culture, but were not powerful enough to withstand attacks by other local tribes. They eventually moved south and settled near the mouth of the Platte River, where they joined forces with the Pawnee tribe. In the early 1880s they moved again and took up residence in Oklahoma.

A little Oto

Lone Chief - Oto

Old Eagle - Oto

Seeing High (Oto)

Standing On The Earth (Oto)

Standing Two - Oto

Wakonda - Oto

White Elk (Oto)

PAWNEE

NOT-CHI-MI-NE

The Pawnee tribe formerly occupied lands in what is now Texas, however, by the early 1540s they had moved to the region of the Platte River in southern Nebraska. They split up into four separate groups in the early 1700s, at which time their population was around 10,000 people. These were the Skidi or Wolf, Grand, Republican, and Tapage (or Noisy) bands. The tribe flourished during this period, and by 1750 they had taken over further territories that extended as far as the Republican River in North Kansas and the Niobrara River in North Nebraska. Although their culture was typical of the Plains Indians, they did, however, have a unique set of myths and rituals. Part of this was the regular sacrifice of a young woman, but this practice had ended by the early 1800s. The Pawnee were fierce warriors who fought constantly with the Sioux and the Cheyenne, but in contrast, they formed close associations with the Oto. They were unusual in that they never fought against the United States government, even when badly provoked. Many Pawnee warriors became scouts for the U.S. Army or worked for the Union Pacific Railroad as guardians against attack by other tribes. Their population was greatly reduced by the combination of wars and epidemics of cholera and smallpox in the 1830s and 1840s. They gave up their lands in Nebraska and moved to a reservation in Oklahoma in 1876.

PIEGAN

NO-TIN
A CHIPPEWA CHIEF

One of the three tribes that formed the Blackfoot or Blackfeet confederacy—the others were the North Blackfoot (Siksika) and the Blood (Kainah)—the Piegan were also known as the Pikuni. The name appears as Peigan sometimes in Canada. An Algonkian people, they had a close alliance with the Atsina (or Gros Ventre) and Sarsi.

A Piegan home

A buffalo-fall (Piegan)

A child's lodge (Piegan)

A grave-house (Piegan)

A medicine pipe--Piegan

A prairie camp (Piegan)

At the water's edge - Piegan

Bringing the sweat-lodge willows - Piegan

Buffalo-stones (Piegan)

Camp by a prairie lake (Piegan)

Camp in the foothills (Piegan)

Crow Eagle - Piegan

Day-dreams (Piegan)

Double Runner - Piegan

Gambler - Piegan

Goldenrod meadows--Piegan

Grizzly-bear brave - Piegan

Idle hour - Piegan

In a Piegan lodge

In the lodge--Piegan

Iron Breast - Piegan

Medicine-bags (Piegan)

Middle Calf - Piegan

PLAIN AND PRAIRIE

Morning Eagle - Piegan

Mountain chief (Piegan)

Navel-amulets (Piegan)

New Chest - Piegan

Old person - Piegan

Overlooking the camp (Piegan)

Painted lodges - Piegan

Piegan dancers

Piegan dandy

Piegan encampment

Piegan girls

Piegan lodge

Piegan war-bonnet and coup-stick

Piegan woman

Piegan

Return to faster's lodge (Piegan)

Return with willows (Piegan)

Running Owl (Piegan)

Substitute sacred head-dress (Piegan)

Sun dance encampment - Piegan

Tearing Lodge - Piegan

The Grizzly-bear (Piegan)

The Whistler (Piegan)

The crier (Piegan)

The pledger (Piegan)

The sun lodge (Piegan)

Three chiefs - Piegan

Travaux - Piegan

Two Bear Woman - Piegan

PLAINS CREE

WO-WAT-KE-SOO-OL

The Plains Cree called themselves Nehiawak, a term which cannot be etymologized. In 1640 the term Kinstinon was mentioned and repeated at frequent intervals in reports over the following twenty years. The priests had not met any tribesmen, however they learned from other Indians that the Cree were a very powerful people. Aside from being nomadic hunters, the Jesuits learned that the Cree fought the Nadouessis and Dakota. From 1656 to 1658, four geographical subdivisions of the Cree were named. The geographical boundaries were Lake Nipigon, west of James Bay, between Lake Nipigon and Moose River, and along the East Main River. This is consistent with the Eastern Cree boundaries outlined in 1656, as defined by Skinner, who visited them some two hundred and fifty years later.

Cree woman with fur robe

Isqe-sis (Woman Small) and child (Cree)

Napeu (Man) (Cree)

Picking blueberries (Cree)

PLAINS OJIBWA

OCHE-FINDEGO

According to their oral tradition, the Ojibwa originally emigrated from the region of the St. Lawrence River in the east, in company with the related Ottawa and Potawatomi peoples. The three tribes separated at what is now Mackinaw City, Michigan, the Ojibwa spreading west over a vast area along the shores of Lake Superior while the two other tribes settled to the south. The Ojibwa, Ottawa, and Potawatomi remained allies through much of their history, united in the Council of Three Fires.

PLAIN AND PRAIRIE

SALISHAN TRIBES INTERIOR

O-HYA-WA-MINCE-KEE,
A CHIPPEWA CHIEF.

A linguistic family inhabiting the north portions of Washington, northern Idaho, western Montana, a small strip of the north west coast of Oregon, and in Canada the south east part of Vancouver Island from Thurlow Island to Sooke Bay, and all the south mainland of British Columbia as far as Bute inlet and Quesnelle Lake, with the exception of that portion held by the Kutenai, although within the Kutenai area, at the Columbia lakes, is a small settlement of Salish. An isolated division of the family, the Bellacoola, had established itself farther north on Dean inlet, Burke channel, and Bellacoola River. The name Salish was originally applied to a large tribe in west Montana popularly known as Flatheads, thence it was finally extended to cover all those speaking a similar language.

SARSI

DKEE-SLAKEE-DUO

The Sarsi (also spelt 'Sarcee') were a hunter gatherer tribe who occupied lands on the upper Saskatchewan River in the early 1800s. Their language belonged to the Athabascan branch of the Nadene linguistic family. The small population of the Sarsi tribe left them vulnerable to attacks by the Cree and other tribes, so they formed an alliance with the Blackfoot people to gain the protection they needed. In 1877 the Candian government managed to persuade them to give up their lands, and in 1880, they moved to a reservation located in Calgary, Alberta. In the early 1990s, the Sarsi people numbered around 800 individuals.

A Sarsi kitchen

A Sarsi tipi

A Sarsi woman

Aki-tanni (Two Guns) (Sarsi)

Ka'ni (Sarsi)

Missi-tsatsa -(Owl Old-woman) (Sarsi)

Typical female physiognomy (Sarsi)

SIOUX (TETON/YANKATONAI ETC)

The Sioux people were a large confederation of native tribes who formerly occupied extensive homelands. A large part of these were distributed from the west bank of the Mississippi River northwards from the Arkansas River almost as far as the Rocky Mountains; not all of this area was open to them, however, as other tribes also lived there. The Northern Sioux lands reached well into Canada, and others lived in the Carolinas, Virginia and in Mississippi along the Gulf coast. There were three major groupings of Sioux tribes. These were the Santee, or Eastern division, who were also known as the 'Dakota', the Middle division or 'Nakota', and the Western division, or 'Lakota'.

The name 'Sioux' is derived from the Chippewa name for them, which translates as 'snake' or 'enemy'. They were hostile to the large numbers of white settlers who came to their lands, and in the end the Sioux tribes were all forced onto reservations. These days their population is over 40,000.

In the land of the Sioux

Invocation - Sioux

Little Hawk - The Teton Sioux

sitting bull

Mountain-sheep hunter - Sioux

Sioux camp

Sioux chiefs

Sioux girl

Sioux hunters

Sioux maiden

The Sioux

Winter camp - Sioux

Wood gatherer - Sioux

sioux american horse

sioux and cheyenne man

sioux buck connor

sioux crazy bull

sioux hump and favorite wives

sioux indians pine ridge agency sd

sioux john crow likes water

sioux oglala black elk with family

sioux oglala chief kickingbear

sioux oglala comes out holy

sioux oglala red cloud

sioux pow-wow

sioux red tomahawk he killed sitting bull

sioux squaws ready for dance

sioux village sweat lodge

WICHITA

OIT-DE-WAB.
A CHIPPEWA CHIEF.

The Wichita (also spelt 'Witchita') were a small agricultural tribe whose ancestors it is believed, came from Arkansas and Louisiana. Over the years they have lived on lands from central Texas to the Arkansas River. When the Spanish explorers encountered the Wichita, they were said to have lived in 'houses made from grass'. This was, in fact, an accurate description as the Wichita built their houses from a domed pole framework which was then thatched with grass. They refer to themselves as 'Kitikitish' which translates as 'racoon eyelids' – this name probably comes from the fact that the men used to tattoo lines on their eyelids. The term 'Wichita' is most likely to come from the tribe's own word 'wits', which means 'men'. Although the tribe were forced out of Texas by white settlers, they never went to war against the United States. In 1850, they settled on a reservation in southern Oklahoma, but during the American Civil War they had to flee the area to avoid the widespread hostilities - they returned home soon after peace was declared. These days there are barely more than 300 living members of the tribe.

A Wichita matron

A Wichita

Braided squash (Wichita)

Ceremonial house (Wichita)

Dancers (Wichita)

Old grass-house (Wichita)

Peeled squash (Wichita)

Peeling pumpkins (Wichita)

Skidi and Wichita dancers

Walter Ross, Wichita

Wichita grass-house

Wichita mortar

Crow Dog (Brule)

Little Dog (Brule)

Little Hawk (Brule)

Ring Thunder (Brule)

American Horse - Ogalala

Big Road's twin daughters (Ogalala)

Blue Horse (Ogalala)

Calico (Ogalala)

Crazy Thunder - Ogalala

Eagle Elk (Ogalala)

Elk Boy (Ogalala)

Fast Thunder (Ogalala)

Good Day Woman (Ogalala)

Good Lance (Ogalala)

He Crow (Ogalala)

His Fights (Ogalala)

Iron Plume (Ogalala)

Kills in Timber (Ogalala)

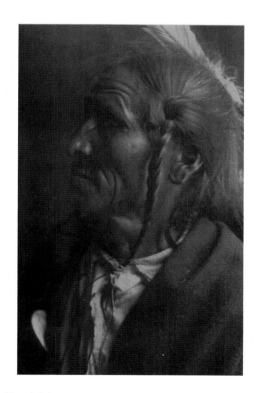

No Flesh (Ogalala)

Ogalala girls

Ogalala war-party

Ogalala woman

Red Cloud - Ogalala

Red Hawk (Ogalala)

Returned Scout (Ogalala)

Shield (Ogalala)

Slow Bull - Ogalala

Standing Bear (Ogalala)

SOUTHWEST (INCLUDING PUEBLOS)

The South-western culture area is comprised of the present day states of Arizona, New Mexico, and parts of southern Colorado and Utah, as well as adjoining parts of Mexico and Texas. There are three sub-regions - the northern area is formed by Colorado, northern Arizona, and northern New Mexico. The western area runs alongside the border between Arizona and California, and the southern area is comprised of southern Arizona, southern New Mexico and adjacent areas of Mexico.

The region's local environments are dictated by the amount of rainfall they receive.

In the wettest areas evergreen trees flourish, and in those which receive less precipitation Piñon pine and juniper can be found. The vegetation in the driest places is mostly scrub, cactus and mesquite.

One of the region's earliest inhabitants were a semi-nomadic civilisation called the Basket Makers. These people started out as primitive hunters - they used a prehistoric weapon called the atlatl to hunt their prey. This is simple throwing device which allows a hunter to send a spear further and faster than is possible by hand alone. Using such weapons they were able to bring down large animals such as bison or deer.

About 3,000 years ago, they started cultivating basic crops such as squash and beans - it is likely that the skills to do so were learned from other local tribes. They also acquired the skills to make pottery, as well as the necessary knowledge to weave objects like baskets and bags. As they got more familiar with these practices, they got better at them, and around 2,700 years ago their agriculture began to get more

productive. They also started using the bow and arrow, which quickly made the atlatl obsolete. The Basket Makers built houses which were dug into the ground and lined with slabs of stone.

As the region dried out around 2,500 years ago, it could no longer support most of the game animals that previously lived there. As a result, the native people of the area were unable to survive by hunting alone. Those that were unwilling or unable to adapt moved away in

search of more productive lands. The tribes that remained developed either predominantly agrarian or nomadic lifestyles. It was around this time that the ancestors of the Pueblo Indians settled in the region.

The name 'Pueblo' is used to refer to any native tribe that lived in the Pueblo-style houses - it does not indicate any specific tribe. These people brought with them a lot of new architectural and agricultural techniques. Their settlements were usually large communal affairs

made from stone or adobe, that were often built partly underground. They typically had several floors or levels that were interconnected by ladders.

The land that was previously unforgiving was able to support these large communities because the new settlers built complicated irrigation systems to water the fields. One of the methods they employed was to construct large storage ditches to catch any rainwater that fell. This meant that the crops were much more productive and

western area can be divided into five main categories. These are the agrarian Pueblo Indians, the Yuman-speaking tribes, the northern nomadic hunter-gatherers, the south-western nomadic hunter-gatherers, and the various Mexican peoples. The Yuman-speaking tribes included the Havasupai, Hualapai, Yavapai, Mohave, Yuma, Cocopah, Maricopa, Pima and Papago peoples. The nomadic hunter-gatherers from the north included the Apache and Navajo, and those from the south-west included the Karankawa and Coahuiltec. Although there were a great many

could therefore feed many more people. This success did not go unnoticed by other tribes in the region, and many of the nomadic ones habitually raided the Pueblo Indians and stole their crops. These wandering tribes were used to gathering whatever they could obtain, and the Pueblo's fields of crops must have presented a tempting target to them. Most of the nomads lived in brush-covered wickiups that could be built quickly and easily as they moved from area to area in search of food.

The many peoples of the south-

different tribes in the area, the predominant language was the Uto-Aztecan branch of the Aztec-Tanoan linguistic stock.

APACHE/APACHE-MOHAVE, OR YAVAPI

The Apache are a large group of associated native Indian tribes - the name is thought to be from a Zuni word for 'enemy', and so does not refer to any one specific people. In all there were around forty or more different groups who were considered to be Apaches, including the Chiricahua Apache, Coyotero, Jicarilla, Kiowa Apache, Lipan, Mescalero, Navaho, Western Apache and the White Mountain Apache. Some of these groups have since become assimilated into other native tribes. It is thought that the Apache's ancestors came to the south-west region around the year 1100 AD. Since then most of the groups have subsisted on a mixture of hunting wild game and gathering things like cactus fruits and the seeds of wild shrubs and grasses. Although they often practised some small-scale farming as well, they would also regularly plunder grain from other tribes. The Apache were renowned for their warrior ways, however, the Eastern Apache were driven from their lands by the Comanche in the early 1720s. The main Apache territories were originally part of Mexico, but once they were acquired by the United States in the mid 1800s, confrontations with white settlers became commonplace. The Apache did their best to stem the flow of these new incomers, but even their fierce resistance was futile in the face of the might of the American military machine. The Apache are still a large group, with over 50,000 living on their extensive reservations in Arizona and New Mexico. Although they retain many of their original cultural practises, they have also managed to adapt to modern business ways and now run successful ranches, timber companies, mineral resource developments and are also involved with tourism.

SOUTHWEST (INCLUDING PUEBLOS)

Alchise - Apache

Among the oaks (Apache)

Apache Nalin

Apache babe

Apache camp

Apache gaun

Apache girl

Apache maiden

Apache medicine-man

Apache reaper

Apache still life

Apache village

Apache-land

Apache

At the ford (Apache)

By the sycamore (Apache)

Chideh - Apache

Cutting mescal (Apache)

Das Lan (Apache)

Desert rovers - Apache

SOUTHWEST (INCLUDING PUEBLOS)

Eskadi - Apache

Filling the pit (Apache)

Geronimo - Apache

Getting water - Apache

Infant burial (Apache)

Lost trail - Apache

Maternity belt (Apache)   Medicine cap and fetich (Apache)

Mescal (Apache)

Mescal camp (Apache)

Mescal harvest (Apache)

Mescall hills (Apache)

Nalin Lage (Apache)

Primitive Apache home

Renegade type - Apache

Sacred buckskin (Apache)

Sand mosaic (Apache)

Scout - Apache

Storm - Apache

Story-telling - Apache

Tenokai (Apache)

The bathing pool (Apache)

The covered pit (Apache)

The fire drill (Apache)

The ford (Apache)

The pool (Apache)

Typical Apache

White River (Apache)

White river valley (Apache)

apache chief geronimo az

apache geronimo in native dress

apache james a. garfield chief

apache marlanetta geronimos wife

apache mescalero women

apache schoolchildren and teacher

arrowheads

geronimo

geronimo

geronimo

wifechild

DIEGUEÑOUS

ONE EA TON EA
CHIEF OF THE OMAHAS

The name Diegueños is not that of a single tribe, but rather a Spanish term that refers to the native Indians of the San Diego region in California. They generally wore little or no clothing, but instead wore highly decorative face and body paint. Jewellery was usually worn in the form of bead necklaces, stone or pottery pendants and hair ornaments. Although they moved around through the year, they were not nomads, since they followed well-organised routes between places where they owned lands. They would travel to these locations to take advantage of the best growing season - once this had passed they would move on to the next site. They practised advanced land management techniques, including controlled burning to reduce the risk from major bush fires, and also used fertilisers to keep the soil in its best condition. They did not rely entirely on agriculture for their food supply - hunting small animals such as rabbits was also commonplace. Some of the original peoples from this group still live in the area, with about 400 of them officially recognised as 'Mission Indians'.

A Campo female (Diegueño)

Communal ceremonial shelter at Capitan Grande (Diegueño)

Diegueño of Capitan Grande

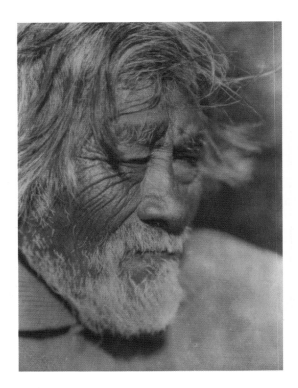

Diegueño of Santa Ysabel

Diegueño woman of Campo

Diegueño woman of Santa Ysabel

Modern rancheria at Santa Ysabel (Diegueño)

Monkey Face - Mesa Grande Diegueño

HAVASUPAI

HO-PO-ETH-LE-YO-HO-LO.

The Havasupai are a tribe of native Indians who live deep in the Havasu Canyon, which is in the north-east part of the Grand Canyon. They are descended from a Yuma tribe who lived in the canyon more than 1,000 years ago. The name breaks down as 'Ha' - meaning water, 'Vasu' meaning blue, and 'pai' meaning people. This refers to the large waterfalls and blue waters that are natural features of the area. The combination of an abundance of water and a hot climate ensured that the Havasupai were able to create effective irrigation systems that helped them grow excellent crops. These provided the mainstay of their foodstuffs - indeed, their culture dictated that the land itself was sacred. The tribal village was only accessible on horseback or by foot along narrow trails. This made their homelands easy to defend. The women became expert basket weavers, a craft they still practise today using cottonwood and willow. There are about 640 Havasupai living today.

Getting water - Havasupai

Havasupai basket maker

Havasupai cliff dwelling

Havasupai matron

Home of the Havasupai   The Canon walls (Havasupai)

HOPI

The Hopi are a group of Pueblo Indians who were originally called Moki, or Moqui. Their culture was that of sedentary farmers who grow the usual native crops of corn, beans and squash. They also grew fields of wheat, cotton, and tobacco, and herd sheep. They inhabited several mesa villages in north-east Arizona, each of which was governed by a chief who also acted as the spiritual leader. The relative isolation of the Hopi meant that they did not have much contact with European settlers until comparatively recently. As a result, they did not suffer from many of the problems that other tribes experienced during the period of white settlement. They did have problem with other native Indians, however. They were often subjected to attacks by other tribes during the 1700s and 1800s - especially by the Navaho. The violence ended when the U.S. Army stepped in, however, even though the Hopi were given a reservation of their own, the Navaho continued to move onto their lands. This is still an ongoing situation, although nowadays the fighting tends to be restricted to the courts. These days there are around 6,700 living members of the Hopi tribe

A cave at Middle Mesa

Antelopes starting for the plaza (Shipaulovi

Approaching the gap at Walpi

Buffalo dance at Hano

Buffalo dance at Hano

Chaiwa - Tewa

Counting the record

Depositing a prayer-stick

Drying pottery

East Mesa pottery

East side of Walpi

Evening in Hopi land

Flute dancers at Tureva Spring

Flute dancers dressing at Kuchina house

Grinding meal

Hano and Walpi girls wearing atoo

Honovi - Walpi snake priest, with Totokya Day painting

Hopi architecture

Hopi maiden

Hopi man

Hopi mother

Hopi woman

Hotavila

Household utensils

SOUTHWEST (INCLUDING PUEBLOS)

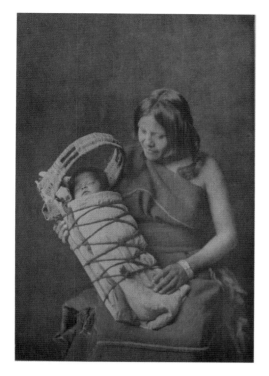

In the cradle-basket

Kachina dolls

Mishongnovi

Offering sacred meal, Mishongnovi flute dance

433

Oraibi plaques

Oraibi snake dance

Piki maker

SOUTHWEST (INCLUDING PUEBLOS)

Potter mixing clay

Pulini and Koyame (Walpi)

Return of a trading party

Shongopavi

435

Sikaletstiwa, Shipaulovi snake chief

Snake priest entering the kiva

Snake priest

Spectators at the snake dance

The plaza at Walpi

The stairway trail at Walpi

The trail to Shipaulovi

The weaver

Walled gardens at Middle Mesa

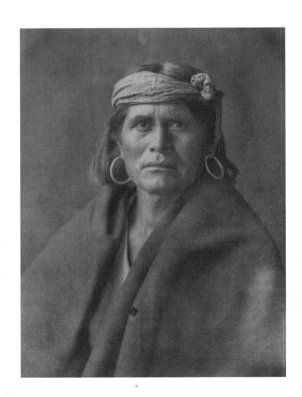

Walpi man

Walpi snake priest

Walpi

hopi baking paper bread.

hopi corn grinding

KERES

The Keres are a group of Pueblo Indians who originally inhabited settlements along the Rio Grande in north central New Mexico. The Keres are one of four tribes of Eastern Pueblo Indians - these are the Keres, Tewa, Tiwa, and Towa. Their homes were carved into the cliffs which were composed of soft volcanic rock called 'tufa'. When the Spanish first explored the area in 1540, they reported that the Keres were distributed across seven Pueblo settlements. A hundred years later it was estimated that they numbered around 4,000. Some of the settlements, such as the Pueblo of Zia, have been inhabited continuously since around the mid 1200s.

MARICOPA

PA - SHE - NINE
A CHIPPEWA CHIEF

The Maricopa are a Yuman tribe that since the 1800s has lived in the region of the Gila River in South Arizona. It is believed that they originally came from the Gulf of California area. Their name comes from the Pima people, whereas they refer to themselves as 'Pipatsje' which means 'people'.

There were originally two different groups of Pima - the Lower Pima and Upper Pima. They lived in domed huts made from pole frames covered with mud and twigs. Even though they were primarily farmers, the Pima were expert archers and also used war clubs and rawhide shields. Although the Pima had many problems with neighbouring tribes, they were friendly towards white settlers, and their villages became regular resting places for pioneers making the long journey to California.

The Maricopa joined with the Pima tribe in the mid 1800s so they could help each other withstand attacks by the Yuma tribe, who were their mutual enemies. This alliance helped them win a spectacular victory against an attack in 1857 by a band of Yuma, Mohave and Yavapai, when 90 out of 93 Yuma warriors were killed. Shortly after this the Papago tribe - who were closely related to the Pima, joined with them. As a people they had also been suffering badly from attacks - in this case by the local Apaches. With help from the Papago and the Maricopa-Pima alliance, the US government were able to force a peace settlement on these violent neighbours.

The Maricopa, Pima and Papago tribes had similar cultures, with farming being their mainstay, although they also gathered foodstuffs from the wild, including mesquite beans and cactus fruit. The women were noted as being especially accomplished basket weavers. In 1859 a reservation was set up for them on the Gila River, and another was later created on the Salt River. These days many members of the tribes are successfully involved in cattle ranching.

By the canal - Maricopa

Captain Charley - Maricopa

Fruit gatherer (Maricopa)

Gathering arrow-brush (Maricopa)

SOUTHWEST (INCLUDING PUEBLOS)

Harvesting cactus fruit (Maricopa)

Havachach Weaving (Maricopa)

Havachachi - Maricopa

Hipah (Maricopa)

Hipah with arrow-brush - Maricopa

Hoo-Man-Hai, Maricopa Indian

Maricopa girl

Maricopa girl

Maricopa group

Maricopa house

Maricopa still life

Maricopa water girl

MOHAVE

PEAH-MUU-KA.
A MOSQUELLE CHIEF.

In the mid 1800s the Mohave inhabited lands on both banks of the Colorado River in Arizona and California, at which time their population was around 3,000 people. When the Spanish explorers arrived in the 1500s looking for gold, the Mohave had the largest settlements in the region, with each village divided into separate clans. The people - who generally had lots of tattoos, were skilled potters who wore very little in the way of clothing. The men usually went about naked, and the women wore small cloths made from rabbit skins. They were fierce warriors when necessary, however, they also travelled vast distances as peaceful traders, exchanging surplus crops for valued items. When they visited the native coastal tribes, for instance, they usually brought back things like seashells. Although the Mohave were initially friendly towards the first white fur trappers, they were appalled at the lack of respect the trappers demonstrated for the animals they killed. They also failed to understand that the creatures they caught were considered Mohave property, and taking them without payment was seen as theft. Consequently, relations soon turned from amicable to extremely violent, and many people were killed on both sides. Eventually matters were sorted out, and in March 1865, the Colorado River Indian Reservation was created by US Government near the southern range of the Mojave lands. Although several hundred people agreed to move to the area, others felt that the lands were too poor to farm effectively, and so remained behind - they became known as the Fort Mohave tribe. A second reservation was eventually granted for them to live on. The tribe fared badly when the authorities tried to impose European-style education upon their children in an attempt to wipe out the native culture. Most of the surviving members now live on the Colorado River Reservation.

An Apache-Mohave woman

An old Mohave

Apache-Mohave homes

Chacha (Mohave)

Hipah (Mohave)

Judith - Mohave.

Mohave chief

Mohave child

Mohave home construction

Mohave man

Mohave mother

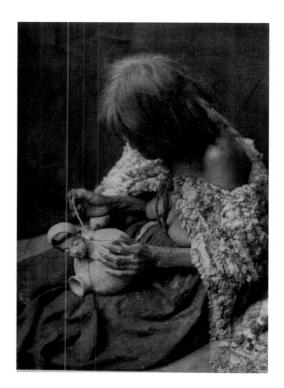

Mohave potter

Mohave still life

Mohave water carrier

Mosa - Mohave

Primitive Mohave

SOUTHWEST (INCLUDING PUEBLOS)

NAVAHO/NAVAJO

PEE-CHEE-KIR,
A CHIPPEWA CHIEF.

The Navaho were one of the tribes that were known as the 'Apache', although they called themselves the D_né', which translates as the 'people'. The term 'Navaho' comes from the Tewa people, and refers to the large tracts of lands they occupied. These are arid areas, and have an average altitude of around 6,000 feet above sea level. The Navaho were relentless enemies of the Pueblo people and local white settlers in New Mexico, who they constantly raided. In order to stop these attacks, the US Army invaded the Navaho lands and killed most of their sheep. This left them unable to feed themselves - on top of this, they also took large numbers of the tribe prisoner. The idea was to demonstrate to the Navaho that they should stop their aggression or face the consequences. In the end the prisoners were released, and they were given replacement stocks of sheep. The concept worked, and the Navaho have not only remained peaceful, but their farms have prospered. They were also very good weavers, and their blankets are still especially highly regarded. The Navaho now occupy a reservation of over nine and a half million acres in north east Arizona, north west New Mexico, and south east Utah. Although these lands are not suited to horticulture, they are good for raising cattle, and as a result the tribe's primary income these days is from ranching.

1865-80 serape navajo blanket

A drink in the desert (Navaho)

A noonday halt (Navaho)

Alhkidokihi - Navaho

Southwest (including Pueblos)

At the shrine - Navaho

Blanket weaver - Navaho

Canyon de Chelly - Navaho

Canyon del Muerto - Navaho

Canyon Hogan (Navaho)

Chief of the desert - Navaho

Cornfields in Canyon del Muerto (Navaho)

Evening in the desert (Navaho)

Gaaskidi (Navaho)

Gaaskidi, Zahadolzha, Haschelti (Navaho)

Haschebaad (Navaho)

Haschelti (Navaho)

Haschelti, Haschebaad, Zahadolzha (Navaho)

Hastobiga - Navaho medicine-man

navajo women

Haschezhini (Navaho)

Haschogan (Navaho)

Into the desert (Navaho)

Jeditoh (Navaho)

Lake Lajara (Navaho)

Morning bath - Apache

Nature's mirror (Navaho)

Navaho Hogan

SOUTHWEST (INCLUDING PUEBLOS)

Navaho Women

Navaho flocks

Navaho medicine-man

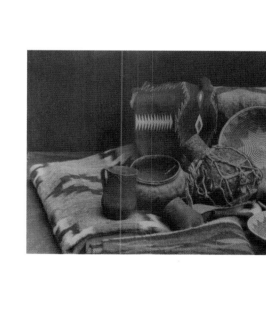

Navaho still life

Nayenezgani (Navaho)

Nayenezgani (Navaho

Nesjaja Hatali - Navaho

Out of the darkness - Navaho

Pikehodiklad (Navaho)

Point of interest - Navaho

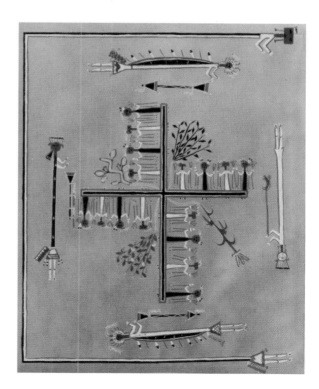

Shilhne'ohli (Navaho)

Sigesh - Apache

Son of the desert - Navaho

The blanket maker (Navaho)

Through the canyon (Navaho)

SOUTHWEST (INCLUDING PUEBLOS)

Tobadzischini (Navaho)

Tonenili (Navaho)

Tonenili, Tobadzischini, Nayenezgani (Navaho)

Under the cottonwoods (Navaho)

Vanishing race - Navaho

Women of the desert - Navaho

Yebichai Hogan (Navaho)

Yebichai dancers (Navaho)

Yebichai sweat (Navaho)

Zahadolzha (Navaho)

navajo blanket red white and black

navajo fort defiance

navajo hogan

navajo indian girl at shiprock

navajo indian rug weaving

navajo indian trading store

navajo indians shiprock

navajo man

navajo men and boy

navajo mother and child

navajo natives of the san juan

navajo race

navajo rug

navajo sand painting

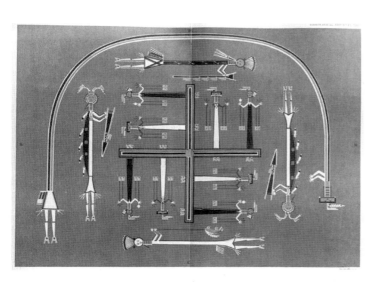

navajo sand painting

navajo silversmith

PAPAGO

Part of the Upper Piman tribes of south Arizona/north Mexico, the Papago were christianized from 1687 and quickly took on first Spanish and then (after the transfer of their territory from Mexico to the US) American ways. They still live in the area in sizeable numbers.

A Papago

Carlos Rios - Papago chief

Gathering hanamh - Papago

Hokak (Papago)

Luzi - Papago

Papago burial

Papago girl

Papago kitchen

PIMA

PETALESHARRO
A PAWNEE BRAVE

The are closely related to the Papago and are part of an old culture that developed canals for irrigation and a successful agricultural life. The advent of the Spanish brought livestock, wheat and Catholicism. Today mainly living on reservations around the Gila and Salt rivers, the Pima now prefer the name O'otain.

A Pima home

Antonio Azul (Pima)

Burden-bearer - Pima

Ceremonial ki (Pima)

Chijako - Pima

Gathering arrow-brush (Pima)

Gathering cactus fruit (Pima)

Isevik (Pima)

Joseph Head (Pima)   Kaviu - Pima

Pima baskets

Pima burial grounds

Pima granaries

Pima ki

PUEBLO DWELLERS

PO-CA-HON-TAS.

The term 'Pueblo' is used to refer to any native tribe that lived in the Pueblo-style houses. The agrarian Pueblo Indians can be sub-divided into those who lived either side of the Rio Grande river. Those from the western side included the Hopi and the Zuni tribes, and those from the east included the Keres, Tewa, Tiwa, Towa, and Piro. The Hopi Indians built their Pueblo houses out of stone and rendered them with clay on both the inside and outside. Their houses had no doors or windows, and could only be entered by climbing through a hole in the roof. The inhabitants used to dry their corn on the roofs of their houses before grinding it into a flour-like meal which was used extensively in their cooking. The women made clay bowls and the men wove cloth textiles. The Anasazi Indians used to build their Pueblo homes onto the sides of cliff faces. These were built of stone blocks held together with a mud-based mortar - the largest ones contained over 200 rooms, and could house more than 400 people. Once the inhabitants had climbed up into their homes, the ladders would be pulled up as well - this gave them a certain degree of protection. Some of the rooms were purely for use by a single family, whereas others were communal. One such room was known as the kiva - this was an underground room that was circular in shape and decorated with paintings of gods. It was exclusively for the use of men, who practised various religious rituals there. It had no doors, and could only be accessed by climbing a ladder through a hole in the ceiling. Around about 1300 AD, construction of the large-scale Pueblo Indian buildings ceased when a period of severe drought weakened the civilisation. Invasions by Navajo and Apache Indians followed, and the Pueblos never regained their former status. The descendants of this population cultivated corn, beans, squash, cotton, and tobacco. They also did a lot of business with their neighbours by trading textiles woven from cotton and yucca fibres as well as grain for buffalo meat from local hunter tribes. Along with growing crops, these people also made fine pottery

Southwest (including Pueblos)

Tewa ('moccasins,' their Keresan name)

POW-A-CHEEK
A FOX CHIEF.

The Tewa are one of the group of four Eastern Pueblo tribes who live in the region of the Rio Grande in northern New Mexico and north-eastern Arizona; they speak languages from the Tanoan linguistic family. The name 'Tewa' comes from the Keres, and translates as 'moccasins'. In the 1600s it was reported that there were about 6,000 Tewa people living in eight pueblo settlements. Each one of the communities developed its own identifiable style of artwork which they incorporated into their basket and textile weaving. The women tend to make the baskets while the men weave blankets, rugs and other fabrics. Many of the living members of the tribe are suffering from low incomes, and unemployment is a big problem. Such issues have caused a lot of anger with the white authorities - this and other social problems still need to be addressed.

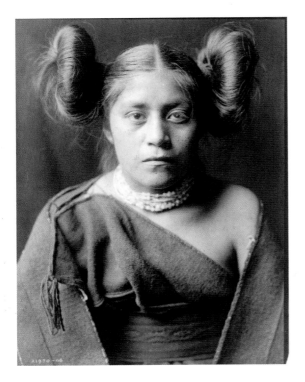

A Tewa girl

A Tewa maiden

Cave-dwellings at Puye

Chaiwa--Tewa

Eagle dancer (San Ildefonso)

Good luck dance by San Juan hunters

Inscription rock

Offering - San Ildefonso

Offering at the waterfall - Nambe

Onate's inscription

Oyegi-aye (Frost Moving), Santa Clara governor

Oyi (Duck White), summer cacique of Santa Clara

San Ildefonso pottery

San Juan pottery

Tablita dance (San Ildefonso)

Tablita woman dancer (San Ildefonso)

TIWA

The Tiwa (also spelt Tigua, Tiguex and Tihua) are a group of native Indians who originally inhabited lands around Isleta, New Mexico, near what is now Albuquerque. They now live in the region of the Ysleta del Sur Pueblo near El Paso, Texas. When the Spanish explorers first reached the Tiwa, they were living in 13 or more settlements. At least three of these contained 200 or more individual houses, and it was estimated that the overall population was around 2,000. Although they were granted lands by the Spanish and Mexican governments - grants which were ratified by the State of Texas, they were still swindled out of their lands by unscrupulous property dealers by the late 1800s. The Tiwa were officially recognised as a tribe in 1967, and put under the jurisdiction of the Commission of Indian Affairs. The surviving members of the tribe currently number around 1,500, some of whom are attempting taking court action to title to some of their traditional lands.

Acoma belfry

Acoma roadway

Among the rocks (Acoma)

At the gateway - Acoma

Cave dwelling near Jemez

Cochiti and Sia pottery

Fiesta of San Estevan, A (Acoma)

Isleta kiva

Jemez architecture

Laguna architecture

Laguna cooking-pot and Acoma water-jars

Native conception of a kopishtaia

Native drawings of Santo Domingo masks

North pueblo at Taos

Old Cochiti

Old house and kiva at Picuris

Paguate watchtower

Picuris harvest dance

Sia buffalo dancer

Sia buffalo mask

Sia war-dancer

Taos water girls

Ti'mu - Cochiti

Tsaiyatsa (Cochiti)

Tsola (Chipmunk), Jemez governor

Tyo'oni Shiwanna mask (Cochita)

Wall-painting for the summer Shiwanna ceremony

Walvia (Medicine Root) (Taos)

WALAPAI

QUA-TA-WA-PEA
COL. LEWIS

The Walapai were a small Yuman tribe who formerly lived in the region of the middle Colorado river. They were hunter gatherers who collected fruits, nuts and berries, and also hunted various game animals. Their name translates as 'pine tree folk', and it is said that they were a hard-working and brave people. The Havasupai were an offshoot of the Walapai, and their languages are closely-related. They fell foul of the American authorities in 1866 as a result of hostilities with local white settlers, and they were interned on the Colorado River reservation. They were eventually allowed to return to their old lands, and were assigned a reservation there. In 1910, they numbered around 500 people, when they owned somewhere around 2,000 horses. At this time they only had a small amount of land under cultivation. Today there are about 1,500 surviving Walapai, many of whom still live on their reservation.

SOUTHWEST (INCLUDING PUEBLOS)

Author's camp, Walapai-land

Pachilawa - Walapai chief

Ta'thamiche (Walapai)

Tokopala (Walapai)

Walapai hunter

Walapai winter camp

YUMA

KANT CHE WAI WE
FEMALE FLYING PIGEON.

The Yuma originally lived where the Gila and Colorado rivers met in south-western Arizona. They were hunter gatherers who also grew crops including corn, pumpkin and beans. The Yuma language family were divided into two distinct groups - one was called the River Yumas - this included the Cocopa, Hakchidhoma, Maricopa, Mojaves, and Yuma. The other group was known as the Upland Yumas - this included the Walapai, Havasupai and Yavapai. The United States government assigned a reservation to the Yuma in 1884 - this was called the Fort Yuma Indian Reservation. These days there are about 3,000 living members of the tribe.

A Yuma home

A Yuma house

A Yuma Man

A Yuma Man

Hapchach (Yuma)

Hwalya - Yuma

Yuma girl. Frontispiece

Yuma maiden

ZUÑI

SB-LOC-TA.
A GREEK CHIEF.

The Zuni were a farming people who are known for their craftsmanship skills in basketry, weaving, pottery and jewellery. Their hand-made products featured elaborate designs, including many different animal motifs. Early Spanish explorers attacked and ransacked the Zuni villages erroneously believing that they had large amounts of gold hidden away - this was as a result of their trying to locate legendary places that were said to be filled with treasure. The Zuni also suffered from attacks by the local Navaho and Apache Indians for many years. Their present day reservations are in McKinley County in western New Mexico, and their population numbers around 9,000.

A Zuñi governor

A Zuñi house shrine

A Zuñi man

Boy and girl columns at Corn Mountain (Zuñi)

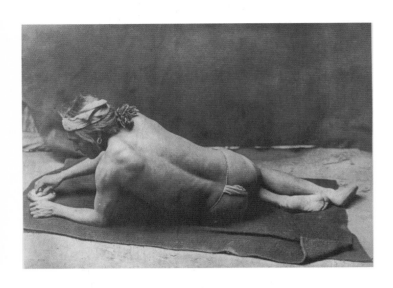

Grinding medicine - Zuñi

Laitsanyasitsa (Zuñi)

Shrine and effigies of the elder war-god

Zuñi woman

Zuñi gardens

Zuñi ornaments

Zuñi village at Ojo Caliente

Zuñi

A Jicarilla feast march

A Jicarilla

Chief Garfield - Jicarilla

Hilltop camp - Jicarilla

Jicarilla maiden

Jicarilla matron

Jicarilla women

Jicarillas

Lone Tree Lodge (Jicarilla)

Vash Gon - Jicarilla

jicarilla apache man

Gathering hasen (Qahatika)

Hasen harvest (Qahatika)

Kiho carrier (Qahatika)

Qahatika girl

Qahatika home

Qahatika man

Qahatika matron

Qahatika village scene

Qahatika water girl

Resting in the harvest field - Qahatika

SOUTHEAST

The South-eastern culture area stretches from the Ohio River down to the Gulf of Mexico; it includes part s of Arkansas, Kentucky, Maryland, Missouri, Oklahoma, Tennessee, Texas, Virginia and West Virginia.

Most of the region has fertile soil and good rainfall - this has resulted in many forests growing in the area. The trees that grow there are mostly southern yellow pine, a species that thrives in the mild, wet climate, although cypress also does well. On the coastal plains there are extensive saltwater marshes, or, as in Florida there are the Everglades. There are many mountains, including those in the Blue Ridge, Smoky and Cumberland Mountain ranges, which are all part of the Appalachians.

The early inhabitants of the region - before the year 500 AD, were semi-nomads who lived a hunter-gatherer lifestyle. They were opportunists who hunted animals with the bow and arrow or with a blowpipe. They fished by poisoning streams or with simple traps, and collected berries, fruit, roots or shellfish depending on what was available at the time. From this date up to around 900 AD, they began to settle and establish themselves as farmers. Around 900 - 1100 AD they started making pottery and building burial mounds - they also took up tobacco smoking and trading on a large scale with other tribes.

The villages they built were mostly sited along the river valleys where there was shelter and the land was more fertile. Most of their houses were built from wattle and daub - this is a process where strips of wood or thin poles are made into a framework and then covered with a mixture of mud and straw. The roofs were made from a variety of different materials, including bark, grass thatch, bamboo, palm fronds or animal hides.

They became adept at growing crops of various kinds of beans, as well as squash, pumpkins and sunflower seeds. The typical pattern was for the men to clear the land and for the women to plant and tend the crops. At other times the men would hunt and the women would gather whatever came to hand. Once the soil was exhausted by having too many crops grown on it, the villages would be relocated to a fresh position.

Many of the tribes lived warlike existences, and to defend themselves they encircled their villages with strong wood and earthen fences called palisades. It was common practice for warriors to be tattooed with symbols representing their particular exploits, and many battles were purely for the purposes of glorification, rather than for any specific military reasons. The settlements usually had religious structures where elaborate ceremonies would be carried out before and after significant battles - both to ask for blessings and to thank the spirits for their assistance.

At more peaceful times other complicated rituals such as sun worship were practised - these usually involved raising spirits, the consumption of special substances with medicine powers, and much dancing. Burial ceremonies were especially highly

regarded, and great efforts were made to honour their ancestors in the process. Certain objects, such as pottery items were often included in the burial mounds - these are known as grave goods, and were believed to help the deceased to make the journey into the afterlife. Harvest ceremonies were considered to have especial relevance, and these often lasted for several days at a time. Thanks were made to the spirit world for giving a good harvest - the most important part for many tribes was the green corn dance.

The native peoples of the region wore clothes made from several different sources - deerskin was popular for shirts, breechcloths, dresses and leggings. Textiles were also made by weaving together beaten plant fibres, or by sewing turkey feathers over a network of twisted fibres. The clothes they made were often highly decorated, and to complement the effect, they also wore body paint to enhance their tattoos.

The social structures of the south-eastern tribal villages were complicated and well organised - most had a chief, who was usually male. He could be head of a single village, a group of villages, or the whole tribe. Each chief would take counsel from several advisors - these could be elder members, shamans or assistants. The Natchez tribe had a form of nobility with a strong hierarchy - the king was referred to as the 'Great Sun', and his family were known as the 'Suns'. Below this were the Nobles and Honoured Men and Women, and the lowest class were the commoners.

SOUTHEAST

When the European settlers arrived, the area was soon over-run with everything from traders to gold prospectors. Some of the traders were slavers - they sent most of their unfortunate captives back to Europe to work for those who could afford them. Other traders exchanged tools and various utilitarian items for buffalo hides and agricultural produce. Missionaries descended on the area and did their best to convert the natives who they saw as heathens into good God-fearing Christians. In doing so they usually also tried to stamp out traditional native religious practices.

While many of the settlers got on well with the natives, others came into conflict with them. This was especially true where land was concerned - many disputes escalated into small scale wars, and people were killed on both sides. As in the other culture areas, the biggest killer of native Indians was disease - smallpox and measles were especially virulent in the south-eastern region.

After the Revolutionary War came to an end several of the south-eastern tribes saw that the Europeans were not going to go away, and so they decided to adopt their ways. They became known as the 'Five Civilised Tribes', and were comprised of the Cherokee, Creek, Choctaw, Chickasaw and Seminole. Amongst other things they wore European clothes and learned to speak English.

After the Indian Removal Act was instituted in 1830 most of the tribes in the area were relocated to the Indian Territories, in what is today the state of Oklahoma. Thousands of natives died during the move - some were shipped and others were forced to march. This infamous journey became known by the Cherokee as 'The Trail of Tears' - a term that was later used to refer to many other native relocations. Some small groups were able to avoid the authorities by hiding in the mountains of eastern Tennessee and western North Carolina.

There were many different languages spoken in the region - some were even specific to individual villages. They include the Atakapan, Nathesan, Yuchian and Chitimachan. Although the remaining tribes have taken to modern ways, most are doing their best to ensure that their tribal traditions are not forgotten. Many tribal children are being taught the ways of their ancestors as part of their education, and this will hopefully foster sufficient interest for this important knowledge to stay alive.

ALABAMA AND COUSHATTA

The Alabama-Coushatta were two separate tribes that now share a reservation in Texas, and after which the State of Alabama was named. Before moving to west Louisiana and eastern Texas in the nineteenth century, they inhabited lands in southern Alabama, where they were members of the Creek Confederacy. They speak a language which is member of the Muskogean branch of the Hokan-Siouan linguistic stock.

APALACHEE

SEQUOYAH

The Apalachee tribe were successful farmers on the Florida panhandle from the Aucilla River westwards, an area known as Apalachee Bay. The land they grew their crops on was extremely fertile, and under their skilled hands it was very productive - this allowed their settlements to prosper and the populations therein to expand. There were probably about 5,000 members of the tribe at its peak. It is believed that the name Apalachee is a Choctaw word for 'people on the other side'. The warlike tribe initially sided with the Spanish, which later resulted in war and defeat at the hands of the British. Over a thousand of them were captured and sold as slaves. Further troubles led to the tribe more or less disappearing from history in the 1800s.

BILOXI

SHA-HA-KA
A MANDAN CHIEF.

The Biloxi have always lived on the fertile lands along the Mississippi River in what are today Mississippi and Louisiana. In the late 17th century, the Tunica tribe first encountered French explorers, who claimed the Indians' homeland for their king. The Tunica soon became valuable, long-term allies of French colonists who settled nearby in the 1700s. After the British forced France to abandon its North American colonies in the 1760s, the Tunica came under control of England, then Spain, and finally the United States.

CALUSA

The Calusa Indians were descended from some of the earliest inhabitants of North America. These people moved into the south-western Florida region around 12,000 years ago. Back then the climate was much colder, and hardwood forests flourished there. Many kinds of large animals were common - these included woolly mammoths, sabre-toothed tigers and giant sloths. The tribe were formerly called the 'Calos', which translates as 'the fierce people'. Although they were hunter gatherers, the Calusa were not the typical simple nomadic peoples that usually go with this lifestyle. Instead they evolved a complex culture that included strong political structures and well developed art forms. It is likely that as the climate warmed up, the seas became more productive and so they depended less on hunting large land animals. The Calusa's dependence on gathering foodstuffs from the sea is reflected in the fact that they are also known as the 'Shell People'. They used shells to make all manner of things, from weapons to tools and jewellery. As a people they were very tall - often up to four inches taller than their European counterparts, and usually had long hair as well. They had good sailing skills, and used canoes carved out from tree trunks. The tribe itself died out in the 1800s, mostly as a result of exposure to diseases like smallpox.

CATAWBA OR KATAPU

SHAU-HAU-NAPO-TINIA.
AN IOWAY CHIEF.

The Catawba tribe formerly occupied part of South Carolina. They were a large and aggressive group who waged a long series of wars against the Cherokee and other local peoples. In the long run these efforts were unsuccessful, and this, combined with several epidemics of smallpox, reduced their numbers considerably. By the end of the eighteenth century they were a very small group. Their language is of the Siouan branch of the Hokan-Siouan linguistic family. There are some surviving members of the tribe who still live in the South Carolina region.

CHEROKEE

The Cherokee tribe played an important part in the history of the United States. As a result they are one of the better known native American groups. It is believed that they originally came from the northern Mexico or Texas region, and at some stage they migrated up to the Great Lakes area. They were then forced out of these lands by wars with the Iroquois and Delaware tribes, and finally settled in the regions of the Allegheny and Appalachian mountains in North and South Carolina, Tennessee, northern Georgia and Alabama. Their first exposure to Europeans was when Spanish explorers encountered them in 1540. Although they lost a large proportion of their population to a massive smallpox epidemic in 1715, their numbers slowly recovered and they are now one of the largest native American tribes in the United States. In the late eighteenth and early nineteenth centuries many thousand Cherokee members moved to lands west of the Mississippi River - this group is known as the 'Western Band'.

CHICKASAW (CHIKASHA)

SPRING FROG
A CHEROKEE CHIEF.

The Chickasaw (also known as the Chikasha) are a tribe that formerly occupied lands in the northern Mississippi region. Although they were closely related to the Choctaw in both language and culture, they fought a long series of wars with them. They were also engaged in more or less permanent wars with the Creek, Cherokee, and Shawnee tribes. In the conflicts between Great Britain and France, the Chickasaw sided with the British, and although the French tried to make peace with them, their attempts failed. After being severely weakened by endless conflicts and outbreaks of disease, they signed up to a treaty whereby they moved to Oklahoma and became one of the Five Civilised Tribes. Their language is of the Muskogean branch of the Hokan-Siouan linguistic family.

CHITIMACHA

STUM MANU.
A FLAT-HEAD BOY.

The Chitimacha occupied lands in the delta region of the Mississippi River and the adjacent Atchafalaya Basin of south-central Louisiana. Up until the mid-1700s, they were considered to be the most powerful native Indian tribe of the northern gulf coast west of Florida. They fiercely contested attempts by the French to colonise Louisiana, and experienced a long war with them. The greatest losses incurred, however, were due to the diseases the French brought with them. It is estimated that in the sixteenth and seventeenth centuries, epidemics of smallpox, measles and influenza killed up to half of the Chitimacha population. The tribe were hunter gatherers who had a wide variety of foodstuffs available to them. The sea provided an enormous bounty, and the land was extremely fertile. The growing season was almost continuous, which meant that their crops were plentiful. On top of this there was a large choice of game animals in the area. This gave them time to develop a complex culture, which included the practise of cranial shaping to flatten their foreheads. They also became expert craftsmen, and were particularly good at basket weaving.

Although they had to relinquish large areas of their original territories to early European settlers, they are one of the few native groups from the Florida region that have managed to retain some of their ancestral lands to the present day. Most of the remaining members of the tribe live on or close to the Chitimacha reservation at Charenton, Louisiana.

CHOCTAW

The main proportion of the Choctaw tribe originally occupied lands in central and southern Mississippi, although there were other smaller groups in Alabama, Georgia, and Louisiana. They were very skilled farmers, with a culture that was closely related to those of the Creek and Chickasaw, even though these tribes were their long-term enemies. In the war between Britain and France over ownership of the North American continent, the Choctaw aligned themselves with the French colonists, and as such did badly when the British came out the eventual winners. In 1832, they were forced to hand over their lands in Alabama and Mississippi, and they moved to the Indian Territories in Oklahoma, where they became established as one of the Five Civilised Tribes.

CREEK OR MUSKOGEE

TAH-BLE [...]

The Creek are a confederacy of Native North American Indians who originally lived in Alabama and Georgia. They were sedentary farmers who often settled along rivers and creeks, and it was for this habit that European traders named them. The Creek Confederacy was formed as an alliance against incursions by aggressive northern tribes by the inhabitants of a fifty or so small towns across the region. The Creek tribesmen were recognised by early European explorers as being tall, proud people who loved to ornament themselves with all manner of decorations. Although they were initially friendly towards the British - partly due to their hostility towards the Spanish, in 1813 they rose up against them in the Creek War. After they were defeated at the battle of Horseshoe Bend they were forced to cede two-thirds of their lands to the United States government. In the end they moved to the Indian Territories in Oklahoma, where they became established as one of the Five Civilised Tribes. These days there are more than 20,000 Creek Indians alive, most of whom still live in Oklahoma.

KADOHADACHO OR CADDO

The Caddo (also spelt 'Caddoe') or Kadohadacho are a native American people who formerly inhabited territories across Louisiana, Texas, Arkansas and Kansas. They were a sedentary tribe with strong religious beliefs that regimented their lives. They lived in small settlements in conical grass huts under a strong class system. Although they were primarily farmers, they were also accomplished horse breeders and traders. During the troubles caused by the arrival of European settlers and the complications that consequently arose, they formed a federation with several other local tribes. The other tribes in this loose alliance included the Arikara, the Pawnee, the Wichita, and others, all of whom had similar cultures. There are some surviving members of the Caddo tribe, some of whom now live on a reservation in Oklahoma.

Natchez

The Natchez tribe were a people who lived along St. Catherine's Creek, which is east of the city of Natchez in Mississippi. Their culture was that of sedentary farmers, however, they were also the most powerful tribe in the lower Mississippi region. The grew crops of corn, beans, and squash, but also hunted for buffalo and deer, as well as for small animals such as rabbits and turkey. They were sun worshippers who had complex social structures, with a class system based on marriage and ancestry. When a chief died, his wives, guards and servants were killed by strangulation as it was believed that they would accompany him in his journey to the afterlife. The Natchez had good relations with the French for many years, but after land disputes war broke out. The French, helped by the Choctaw heavily defeated the tribe, and many of the survivors were sold into slavery. Some managed to avoid capture though, and settled among the Chickasaw, who were their allies. As a result, the tribe intermarried so much that by the beginning of the twentieth century it had more or less disappeared as a distinct entity.

INDIANS OF OKLAHOMA

The State of Oklahoma has a particular significance to native American Indians, for it is where many of them ended up in the government appointed Indian Territories. When the first Europeans arrived as explorers, there were several different groups already living there. These included the Osage, Kiowa, Arapaho, Wichita, and Caddo peoples. Most of them were hunter gatherers who hunted buffalo when the opportunity arose - for this was before the horse was introduced, and farmed the land the rest of the time. The plants they grew were primarily corn, beans, and squash. On the whole the explorers were Spaniards looking for gold - the first arrived in the sixteenth century. After this came the French, who claimed the land for their king. They started out by exploring and then in the 1700s, they built trading posts to profit from furs and other products bought from Indian hunters.

In 1800 the area was given by the Spaniards to the French, and then in 1803 it was sold to the United States. Since the lands in the east were more desirable to the European settlers, the government had to move the Indians to somewhere else, and Oklahoma seemed ideal for the purpose. It was a long way from anywhere, and no-one else wanted to live there at the time. Five of the main tribes were forced into moving there from their homelands in the east. This journey has entered the rolls of infamy as the 'Trail of Tears', since of the 75,000 who started out, many thousands died of disease, hunger and cold before they reached their destination. These groups were those who became known as the 'Five Civilised Tribes' - they were the Seminoles, Creeks, Chickasaws, Choctaws, and Cherokees.

Buffalo

Peyote drummer

Story of the Washita

The Washita

OKMULGEE

TRIPOOCHEE BARNARD
AN ULTER WARRIOR.

The Okmulgee tribe formerly occupied lands in the region of the Chattahoochee River, Russell County, Alabama. The name comes from the Hitchiti language, and means "where water boils up" - this may well refer to the local natural features called Indian Springs in Butts County, Georgia. They were a small group at the best of times, and in the mid 1700s there were only 20 - 30 adult males in the tribe. By the early 1820s this had risen to a total - including women and children of about 220. They were closely associated with the nearby Chiaha and Osochi tribes. The Okmulgee language came from the Muskhogean linguistic family.

SEMINOLE

TISH CO HAN.
A SEMINOLE CHIEF.

The Seminole was a group of affiliated native Indian tribes who began joining together in the early eighteenth century to avoid white enslavement and land disputes and associated problems. Other tribes continued to join up with them until the beginning of the nineteenth century. They originated in Georgia, Alabama and South Carolina, and finally settled in Spanish-held north and central Florida. The name is from the Muskogee word "simano-li," which means runaway. When the United States government tried to take their new lands as well, they fought back in what became known as the First Seminole War. Eventually a treaty gave them lands east of Tampa Bay, but these were then taken away by the Payne's Landing Treaty of 1832. Due to double-dealing by the United States authorities, the tribe reacted angrily and started the Great Seminole War. After seven years of conflict and many thousands of deaths, the war finally came to an end in 1842. Although some members of the tribe were allowed to remain in Florida, most of them were removed to the Indian Territories in Oklahoma, where they became established as one of the Five Civilised Tribes. These days there are about 12,500 members of the tribe, most of whom still live in Oklahoma.

TAENSA OR NATCHEZ

TO KA CON
A SIOUX CHIEF.

The Taensa (Taenso, Tahensa, Takensa, Tenisaw, Tenza, Tinza) Indians were Muskhogean-speaking Indians who originally lived near the Mississippi River in northeastern Louisiana. In the early nineteenth century, after they had moved to southwestern Louisiana, the Taensas petitioned the Spanish government for lands in southeastern Texas. They were granted permission to settle between the Trinity and Sabine rivers, but the move was never made.

TUNICA

TEHI-ZUN-HAU-KAU
A WINEBAGO.

The Tunica and Biloxi tribes settled long ago on the rich farming lands of the Mississippi River in what today are the states of Mississippi and Louisiana. They were hunter gatherers who grew corn and squash and also collected many different kinds of foods from the wild. The women gathered fruits, berries, seeds and nuts, and they also dug for various roots and tubers. The men hunted for game animals like deer and buffalo, from which they gained meat as well as hides and other important things like fat and sinew. The villages they lived in were composed of round huts built from vertical posts through which canes were woven - these were then rendered with clay and topped with thatched roofs. The huts themselves were around an open central area where feasts, dances and games would be held - there would also usually be a temple sited nearby. Religion played a strong part in the culture of these tribes, with the sun being considered an important deity. Most of the Tunica and the Biloxi tribes joined together in the early 1800s, and several other local groups also merged with them over the next few decades. In 1981, they were officially recognised by the United States government as the Tunica-Biloxi tribe.

NORTHEAST

The region which makes up what is referred to as the North-eastern culture area comprises much of the North Atlantic coast. The southernmost point is just south of the Ohio river, and it stretches north as far as the temperate parts of southern Canada. It then reaches inland across the Appalachian Mountains and as far west as the Mississippi River Valley. The Great Lakes mark the northern border in the interior, with Virginia and North Carolina delineating the southern edge.

This large area contains many major rivers, including the St. Lawrence, Ohio, Wabash, Hudson and Susquehanna, and lakes - especially those known as the Great Lakes. Almost all of the region is forested with mature trees - these are both coniferous and deciduous. Where the conifers proliferate there is not much in the way of wildlife for humans to hunt, but the deciduous woodlands support all manner of suitable target animal species. The main focus was upon deer, which provided food in the form of meat, clothing and shelter from skins, and vitally important binding materials from sinew. These were used for making clothes, shoes, and most importantly, weapons.

Since finding enough food and shelter to survive was relatively straightforward in this region, many different tribes settled there, and archaeological remains suggest that the first native settlers arrived around 9,000 years ago. Back then the climate was warm, but around 3,000 years ago this changed, and it became more or less what it is today - a temperate zone, with cold - often freezing, winters and warm summers.

Although there was plenty of food to be had, it had to be searched for, so most of the tribes that settled in the region were semi-nomadic. They had permanent homes in large villages, as well as temporary structures for when they were out hunting or gathering. They assembled these shelters from whatever brushwood was to hand at the time.

When they were away from their villages, the Algonquian-speaking tribes such as the Chippewa and the Abenaki would gather nuts, berries and wild grains whilst others went hunting small animals like deer or rabbits. The tribes that lived along the coast would also fish with spears, traps, hooks and nets, as well as gather shellfish along the shoreline. Fishing excursions were made more successful with the advent of the birch-bark canoe - these were lightweight and very manoeuvrable, which made them ideal for the task.

Some of the tribes people - generally the women, supplemented their supplies by growing crops of corn, sunflowers, beans and squash. This was done when the fields were suitably close to sources of fresh water. Many seed-bearing plants were also grown - the seeds were then collected and stored. When needed, they were ground into flour and made into bread or other foodstuffs. The cooking utensils were made of wood or simple black pottery.

The abundance of trees meant that there was always plenty of firewood for cooking and keeping warm, as well as for more structural purposes such as building shelters - be they temporary or permanent. Different tribes had different solutions to the issue of housing - some, such as the Iroquois built substantial communal long houses, with

separate areas for each family. Often there would be several fireplaces, and to allow the smoke to escape there would be a series of smoke holes in the roof. The communal long houses of the North-eastern region would be up to 50 feet long, however, some tribes also build massive ceremonial ones. These could be anything up to 200 feet long and 30 feet high. The roofs and walls of these structures were generally made weather proof with large pieces of tree bark.

Most of the Algonquian groups, however, went for villages of dome shaped wigwams made of poles and covered with bark or skins, instead of long houses. In order to protect themselves against attack by enemies or animals such as bears and mountain lions, most villages were also surrounded by tall wooden fences made from sharpened poles up to 12 feet high.

For the native tribes in the region, the preferred choice of material for clothes was generally deerskin, as it is warm, soft, supple and comfortable to wear. They used it to make leggings, shirts, breechcloths and dresses. Many people also painted their faces, and the men often shaved both sides of their heads. Grease made from bear fat was commonly used to condition the hair.

Like most native American Indians, the tribes people of the North-eastern region were very spiritual. They believed there was a strong link between man and nature, and the sight of Europeans cutting down entire forests and killing large numbers of animals with no regard upset them deeply. They saw connections between the world around them and the spirits more or less everywhere. Different tribes had different

interpretations for how certain animals interacted with the spirits. It was thought that shamans - medicine men, could summon helper spirits to help cure diseases or bestow good luck on hunting expeditions.

When the first European settlers arrived on the North Atlantic coast the first natives they met were from the North-eastern tribes. Many of these new arrivals had little or no idea as to how to survive - unbelievably they had not bothered to learn before they left to cross the ocean. Some of these people owed their lives to the local native Indians who showed them how to grow crops and deal with other vital tasks. This positive association did not last, however, and before long disputes broke out over land ownership - this often resulted in serious fighting.

When Britain and France started battling for control over North America most of the tribes in the region ended up fighting for one side or the other. In many cases this meant that the various native tribes ended up in conflict with each other, as well as their European foes. The Iroquois League sided with the British, and this assistance meant the French were forced out of most of the region. The Huron and many Algonquian-speaking tribes, however, sided with the French. When the Revolutionary War broke out, the Iroquois League started to collapse as some groups sided with the British and others with the colonists. The league finally ended not long afterwards as a result of disease and other problems.

The Iroquois have managed to retain their ancestral lands, although many of the other tribes from the North-eastern region are now located in Oklahoma and neighbouring states as a result of US government relocation.

ABENAKI

TOMUSICK.

The Abenaki tribe (also spelt Abnaki, Abanaki, Abinaki and Abenaqui) used to occupy lands in what are now the States of Maine, New Hampshire, and Vermont, although their tribal legends suggest that they originally came from the south-west. The tribe were hunter gatherers who grew crops, hunted and fished depending on the season. They lived in small villages of conical huts surrounded by strong wooden fences. The Abenaki sided with the French in the Colonial Wars, and as such fought the British for many years. When they were eventually defeated, they retreated into Canada, along with several other related tribes. These included the Malecite, Passamaquoddy, Pennacook, Penobscot, as well as various other smaller groups. The tribal name Abenaki came from their French allies, although it should actually be 'Wabanaki' or 'Wobanaki', this Indian word translates as 'those living at the sunrise'.

ALGONKIN OR ALGONQUIN

The Algonquians (also spelt Algonkians, Algonquins or Algonkins) were a small group of native American Indians who formed alliances with the early French explorers and settlers. They fell foul of the Iroquois, against whom they were no match, and in the 1600s their tribe was fragmented across parts of southern Canada. It was more or less at this time that the tribe as an entity ceased to exist. Their language was part of the Algonquian-Wakashan linguistic family.

BROTHERTON OR BROTHERTOWN

TUSTENNUGGEE EMATHLA

The Brothertown (also spelt Brotherton) were a group that was formed by Christian Indians from the New England and Long Island, New York, areas. The Christian religion became popular with several tribes, including the Mohegan, Montauk, Narragansett, Niantic, Pequot, Tunxis, and Wangunk. This movement, which occurred during the 1740s in New England, was known as the 'Great Awakening'. As a consequence of their new found sensibilities, they did their best to avoid the rampant alcoholism and other social problems that were rife amongst the settlements of North America. In the 1770s two Mohegan ministers led a large group of New England tribal families to new homelands in the territories of the Oneida tribe in north central New York. The name Brothertown was used because they wanted to live as brothers under Christianity. Shortly afterwards the Stockbridge tribe also moved to Oneida lands, however, the pressures from European settlers did not abate. Their constant demands for new farmlands meant the territories were badly eroded - much of this was achieved by deception and double-dealing. This left them with little option but to move to new lands where they would no longer be under threat. They chose to move to Wisconsin, and following the signing of the appropriate treaties they bought most of the western shores of Lake Michigan. The move began in the early 1830s, however, it was not long before ever increasing numbers of white settlers also moved to the area. They brought with them the very problems the Brothertown had been trying to leave behind. Once the settlers realised that the area was good farmland, the Brothertown came under a lot of pressure to relinquish their lands. Many sold their farms and moved off to other areas, which resulted in their becoming ever more scattered over the next hundred years. Land disputes concerning their original homelands in New York and attempts to regain federal recognition for the tribe continue to this day. There are somewhere around 1650 tribal members alive today.

CAYUGA

WAA PA SHAW
A SIOUX CHIEF.

The Cayuga Nation are referred to by many different names, including the later term 'Seneca-Cayuga'. The name Cayuga means the 'people of the marsh'. The name Seneca comes from the Iroquoian language, and translates as "people of the standing rock", although they were also known as the 'keepers of the Western door'. The Cayuga moved to Ohio after the American Revolution, where they settled on a reservation alongside the Sandusky River. Both the Cayuga and the Seneca tribes banded together with others (the Conestoga, Mingo, Mohawk, Oneida, Onondaga, Shawnee and Tuscarora) under the Iroquois Confederacy. Eventually the entire alliance ended up living on the Indian Territories in the State of Oklahoma. They experienced many problems as a result of border disputes, and during the American Civil War there were many battles on their lands which resulted in many of them fleeing to safety elsewhere. These days most of the tribe's members still live in Oklahoma.

DELAWARE

WAA-TOP-E-NOT.

The Delaware peoples were not a single tribe, but an alliance of several closely associated ones. In the 1600s they inhabited lands in the Delaware, New Jersey, eastern Pennsylvania, and south-eastern New York areas. The name 'Delaware' was applied to them by the English settlers, since they lived in the region of the Delaware River; they referred to themselves, however, as Lenni-Lenape. The alliance itself was based on the main sections - the Munsee (meaning 'wolf'), the Unalachtigo (meaning 'turkey'), and the Unami (meaning 'turtle'). In the days of the early settlers, they did a lot of trading with the Dutch. As land pressures developed, they sold much of their homeland and moved inland to the Susquehanna valley. The Iroquois attacked them in 1720, and as a result they were forced to move again - this time to Ohio. After various troubles with the European settlers, they were defeated and they had to hand over their lands once more. After travelling extensively, they were eventually moved to the Indian Territory where they settled with the Cherokee.

FOX OR MESQUAKIE

WA-BISH-KEE-PE-NAS.
The White Pigeon.

The Sac and the Fox tribes were two separate groups that were close allies for many years. The Sac, who are sometimes referred to as the Sauk lived as skilled farmers who participated in raiding parties against other tribes from time to time. The Fox, who are also known as the Mesquaki, were fierce warriors who waged a long-standing war against the Ojibwa. They originally occupied lands in the Saginaw Bay area in east Michigan, but as a result of their raiding parties were driven out of the region by the Ottawa and Neutral tribes. Both the Sac and the Fox moved north into what is now the state of Wisconsin. It was not long before they were at war with the French, as well as with the Sioux and the Illinois tribes. The French finally decided they had taken enough harassment, and they commenced to wipe out the Fox. This reduced their numbers to such an extent that they were no longer a significant force. It was at this time - the early 1730s, that they banded together with the Sac on a permanent basis. Since then, the two tribes have been known as the Sac and Fox. In the early and mid 1800s, their aggressive ways started the Black Hawk War, after which they were forced to move away - they wandered for some time and finally settled on reservations in Iowa, Kansas, and Oklahoma.

HURON OR WYANDOT

WA . BAUN . SEE,
A POTTAWATOMIE CHIEF.

The Huron tribe were so named by early French explorers and settlers - it means 'rough', and refers to the bristled haircuts worn by the warriors. The tribe called themselves the Wendat, which is an Iroquoian word which translates as 'islanders' or 'dwellers on a peninsula'. When they weren't fighting, the tribal members were good farmers who grew the typical crops of the native American Indians - corn, squash and beans. They also cultivated tobacco and sunflowers in the fields around their palisaded villages. In the 1600s they fought a long war with the Iroquois - this came to a head when an epidemic of malaria weakened the Huron, and at the same time the Dutch armed the Iroquois with guns. The Huron were badly defeated and had to flee - some went south to the Neutral Nation. Others took off to the south-west to the Tobacco Nation or even went north into Canada to seek protection from the French. This cost their new hosts dearly - the Iroquois invaded both the Neutral and Tobacco Nations, and more or less wiped them out. The survivors settled in Wisconsin and Illinois, where they fell foul of the Sioux. This forced them to move yet again, and they ended up living in villages near Detroit and at Sandusky, Ohio. Those who had taken refuge in Canada were given a small reservation to live on, where some still live to this day. The Huron fought with the British in the American Revolution and in the War of 1812 - they called the tribe the 'Wyandotte' or 'Wyandot'. Although they had their lands confirmed by the government authorities, they sold them off and in 1842 moved to Kansas, in what is now called Wyandotte County. This was not a lasting solution, however, as white settlers kept taking more and more of their lands. In the end they bought some land from the Seneca Tribe in the Indian Territory in Oklahoma, where many of their approximately 3,600 descendants still live.

ILLINI OR ILLINOIS

WA-EM-BOESH-KAA

The Illini - also known as the Kaskaskia, were a federation of several native American Indian tribes - this was composed of the Cahokia, Kaskaskia, Michigamea, Moingwena, Peoria, and Tamaroa tribes. The name Peoria translates as "he comes carrying a pack on his back". In the 1600s, these peoples inhabited lands in the south Wisconsin and north Illinois areas, as well as parts of Iowa and Missouri. At this time there were about 6,500 members in total, however, within a hundred years, wars with the Sioux, Fox, and Iroquois reduced this figure to around 2,000. Things got worse when a tribal member assassinated Pontiac, who was a famous chief of the Ottawa tribe. The Lake tribes blamed the Illini, and program of extermination began - by the end of the eighteenth century there were only about 150 members left. In 1833 these last survivors sold their lands in Illinois and moved to a reservation in Miami County, Kansas. Today the descendants of these people live on a reservation in north-east Oklahoma which they purchased from the Quapaw and Shawnee tribes.

IROQUOIS

WA . KA'WN.
A WINNEBAGO CHIEF.

The Iroquois Confederacy which was formed around the fourteenth century was initially composed of five different groups, hence their title of 'Five Nations'. These were the Cayuga and Oneida (who were known as the 'Younger Brothers'), the Mohawk (who were called the 'Eastern Doorkeepers'), the Onondaga (known as the 'Firekeepers') and the Seneca (the Western Doorkeepers'). They were later joined by the Tuscarora, who were accordingly titled the 'Adopted Brothers'. The Iroquois had a complicated political system, and were the most powerful native Indian military force in North America. When the Huron pushed them too far, the Iroquois used Dutch guns to hunt them and their allies down however far they fled. These conquests included the Huron in 1649, the Tobacco and the Neutral Nations in 1650, the Erie in 1656, the Conestoga in 1675, and the Illinois around the year 1700. The borders of their territories were only formed due to the presence of other powerful tribes - in the west this was by the Ojibwa, in the south by the Cherokee and Catawba, and in the north by the French.

KICKAPOO

WAKECHAI,
A SAUKIE CHIEF.

In the 1600s the Kickapoo (also spelt Kikapoo or Kikapu) inhabited lands in the south-west Wisconsin area. Although their culture was based on those of the other Eastern Woodlands tribes - in other words an agricultural and gathering lifestyle, their location - which bordered the Plains Indians, meant that they also developed into accomplished buffalo hunters. When the Illini tribes incurred the wrath of the Kickapoo and their allies, the Ojibwa, Ottawa, Potawatomi, and Sac and Fox, the Illini were heavily defeated. Their lands were then divided up and the Kickapoo took over the region around central Illinois. They were later forced to relinquish these territories, and they travelled to Missouri and then on to Kansas. Many disliked the reservation they were assigned, and moved to Mexico in around 1852. In order to feed themselves there, they constantly raided American settlements along the border. This forced the United States government to offer the Mexican Kickapoo a reservation in Oklahoma - after successful negotiations some settled there in 1873-1874. The remaining populations live in Kansas, Oklahoma, and Chihuahua, Mexico.

MAHICAN OR MOHICAN

WA. KAWN. HA. KA.

The Mahican Confederacy were of the Eastern Woodlands culture; they consisted of several groups, one of which was the Mohegan. The similarity of names often leads to confusion, especially as both groups are sometimes called 'Mohicans'. The Mohegan tribe were the eastern branch of the Mahican Confederacy; in the early 1600s they inhabited lands that covered most of south-western Connecticut. At this time the Mohegan did not exist as a separate group - they were part of the Pequot tribe (whose name means 'destroyers'), however, they split in two after a rebellion by an internal faction against an unpopular chief called Sassacus, by what became the Mohegan. He was finally deposed when the Pequot killed an English trader. The British retaliated, and some 500 members of the tribe were killed in the ensuing battles. The survivors escaped in various directions, with one group led by Sassacus being captured and killed or sold as slaves by the Mohawk. Those who were not caught settled where they could amongst the other tribes of southern New England. The rest of the Mahican Confederacy fared little better - the Mohawk used guns provided by the Dutch to defeat and disperse them. A few Mahican still survive, with most of them living in Connecticut and Wisconsin.

MENOMINI OR MENOMINEE

The Menominee (also spelt Menomini) were people who had a gatherer culture. Their main foodstuff was wild rice which they gathered in large quantities. Their name comes from the word 'manomin', which is Algonquian for 'wild rice'. In the 1630s they inhabited the fertile lands at the mouth of the Menominee River in Wisconsin and Michigan. Although they had peaceful relations with the white settlers, they fought bitter wars with many of the other local tribes who wanted to seize the places where the wild rice grew so successfully. They managed to hold on to these homelands until 1854 when they were moved to the Menominee Reservation on the Wolf River in north central Wisconsin. The tribe became independent of Federal Control in 1961.

MICMAC

The Micmac (also spelt Mi'kmaq, Mikmaq, or Mikmak) inhabits lands across Nova Scotia, Cape Breton Island, Prince Edward Island, Newfoundland, and New Brunswick. Since their lands were surrounded by water they became very skilled canoeists, and they obtained most of their foodstuffs from fishing or hunting from boats. The first consistent contact they had with Europeans was with French missionaries in the early 1600s. As a result they became allied to the French - indeed, their name translates as 'allies'. They did not suffer the usual tribulations that most of the other native peoples endured, and the tribe is still flourishing, albeit in a very different form. These days, the tribe earn most of their income from farming.

MOHAWK

WESH-CUBB
A CHIPPEWAY CHIEF.

The Mohawk have had a turbulent history in the years since the Europeans arrived on the continent. The name was given to them by the Algonquin Nation, and translates as 'they who eat animate things', or 'man-eaters'. They called themselves 'Kaniengehaga' or 'Kanien'kehaka' which means 'people of the place of the flint'. They were the most easterly of tribes of the Iroquois Confederacy, and during the warmer parts of the year they lived along the St. Lawrence River. When it got colder, they moved to the 'Mohawk Valley' in Central New York State where they had permanent long houses. These could be anything up to 120 feet long, and were covered in tree bark. There are three clans of Mohawk - these are known as the Bear, Wolf, and Turtle clans. They were a warlike people who fought most of the other tribes in the region. These wars affected their population badly - at the end of the fifteenth century they almost completely disappeared. When the Dutch gave them guns to help hunt beaver they also used them to good effect to defeat their enemies. The Mohawk had a ritual of cooking and eating their prisoners - the common people were allowed to eat the limbs and torso, but the chiefs ate the heart and the head. The tribe fought for the British in the Revolutionary War, and afterwards were given lands in Canada by the British Government. Those Mohawk peoples who remained in the United States were driven out by the Oneida in 1777. Most of the surviving members still live in Canada.

OJIBWA OR CHIPPEWA

A WINNEBAGO.

The Ojibwa are the same group as the Chippewa - these are not, as it might seem, different names, but different spellings of the same word; this confusion is because of the unusual native pronunciation. Ojibwa can also be spelt Ojibway, Ojibwe and Ojibwemowin. The Northern Ojibwa formerly inhabited lands on the shores of Lake Superior, Wisconsin. Here they were a hunter gatherer peoples, who grew corn and squash, collected wild rice, and hunted deer or fished the rivers and lakes. The rich source of wild rice on their lands were envied by both the Sioux and the Fox, and as a result the Ojibwa were in a more or less permanent state of war with them. Fortunately for them, they managed to get hold of guns before their enemies, and around 1690 they forced the Fox out of the region. Shortly after this they expelled the Sioux, and expanded their territories as far afield as central North Dakota. The Ojibwa who moved to this new area became known as the Plains Ojibwa. They also obtained large tracts of land from the Iroquois after defeating them, which meant that by the mid 1700s they became one of the largest tribes in North America. At this time their population was around 25,000. The tribe signed a treaty with the United States government in 1812, since when they have lived on reservations in Michigan, Wisconsin, Minnesota, and North Dakota. These days there are also something like 50,000 Ojibwa living on reservations in Canada.

ONEIDA

YAHA-HAJO.
A SEMINOLE CHIEF.

The Oneida are an ancient people who formerly inhabited lands between the St. Lawrence River and the Pennsylvania border. They were one of the tribes that made up the Iroquois Confederacy, and were, like the Mohawk, divided into three clans - the Bear, Wolf and Turtle Clans. They were farmers who would also hunt buffalo and other game animals when the opportunity was there. When the European settlers arrived, the Iroquois were quick to exploit the chance to obtain modern items - especially the gun, by trading beaver furs with them. In the Revolutionary War the other members of the Iroquois Confederacy had fought for the British. The Oneida, however, had sided with the Americans, and although they were on the winning side they were expelled from their lands. The United States government gave them a treaty to protect their lands in New York, but as was usual back then, the deals were duplicitous, and their 6 million acres were soon reduced to almost nothing. Many members of the tribe moved away to Canada and Wisconsin in the 1830s, however, a few decided to remain. Ever since then, they have tried to get legal recompense for having their ancestral lands taken from them - the affair is ongoing, and will undoubtedly continue for some time yet.

OTTAWA

The Ottawa tribe formerly inhabited lands across the southern part of Michigan, in the area of the Grand River, as well as more in Ohio and Indiana. Their name comes from the Algonquian word 'adawe', which means 'to trade', and it refers to the fact that they bought and sold items across a wide area. They had especially good trade connections with both the Ojibwa and the Potawatomi. In the mid 1600s the tribe were forced to move west to the Green Bay, Wisconsin area due to the onset of wars. By 1700 they had spread all over the region, from southern Wisconsin to northern Illinois, to Lake Huron, Lake Erie and from Detroit eastward to Pennsylvania. The Ottawa had a powerful chief called Pontiac who was determined to stop the British taking all their lands. In 1763 he started a war, but was not successful in getting all the other native tribes to join in with him. Realising he could not win, he finally made peace in 1765. The tribe were forced to hand over their lands in Ohio in 1831. Although they were given new territories in Kansas, these were soon taken from them, and they were allotted land in the Indian Territories in Oklahoma instead, where their descendants still remain.

PEQUOT

YOUNG MA HAS KAH
CHIEF OF THE IOWAYS

Once resident in Connecticut, the Pequot were decimated in 1637 by a force made up of the English and two Indian tribes—the Mohegan and Narragansett. Few were left after the captives were sold into West Indian slavery, and those that remain today live near Ledyard. They are one of the few groups that can claim ancestry back to the original inhabitants of southern New England.

SAULTEAUX AND NORTHERN OJIBWA

Originally living in the eastern woodlands, the Saulteaux or Northern Ojibwa moved northwest both because of European population pressure and also the lucrative fur trade. A sizeable tribe (over 30,000 were reported in 1978) those that are left are difficult to differentiate from other Ojibwan and Cree peoples.

SAUK

The Fox and the Sauk are two closely related, but separate, tribes which in 1600 occupied the eastern half of lower Michigan between Saginaw Bay and Detroit. Both of their oral histories tell of an earlier time when they migrated from the Atlantic coast via the St. Lawrence River. When this happened is unclear. The Sauk lived around Saginaw Bay (which is named from them), while the Fox were just to the south and west. Driven from their homeland during the 1640s, the Fox resettled in central Wisconsin. The Sauk crossed over to the upper peninsula near the Mackinac Strait and moved into the headwaters of the Wisconsin River west of Green Bay. Except for the two-years (1710-12) the Fox lived near Detroit, neither tribe ever returned to Michigan. They remained in Wisconsin until 1734, when both were driven across the Mississippi River into eastern Iowa by the French.

SHAWNEE

WAR DANCE OF THE SAUKS AND FOXES.

The Shawnee tribe formerly inhabited lands in Ohio, although by the mid 1600s the tribe had split in two - one part living in western South Carolina and the other in northern Tennessee. They continued to move around separately for about a hundred years, until they joined up again in the mid eighteenth century in Ohio; at this stage their population was around 1500. They were a warlike tribe who took part in most of the wars in the north-west region. In 1795 a treaty forced them to give up their territories in Ohio and relocate to Indiana. They tried staging an uprising at the beginning of the nineteenth century, but this failed and they were once again forced to move - firstly to Missouri, then to Kansas, and they ended up in Oklahoma. These days about 2,250 Shawnee still live on reservations in Oklahoma.

INDEX

T

U

W

Y

Z